Let's Explore the Desert

FAMILY

Go Guide!

Let's Explore the Desert

FAMILY

Go Guide!

by Doris Evans

Arizona-Sonora Desert Museum Press

Dedicated to the memory of my parents who encouraged my love of nature, and to my husband, Doug, who shares that love today.

Published in the United States by
Arizona-Sonora Desert Museum
2021 N. Kinney Road,
Tucson, Arizona 85743
www.desertmuseum.org

This book is available at quantity
discounts for educational, business,
or sales promotional use. For further
information, please contact:
Arizona-Sonora Desert Museum Press
2021 N. Kinney Road
Tucson, AZ 85743
(520) 883-3028
asdmpress@desertmuseum.org

Editor Steven Phillips
Book and Cover Design Jackie Stein

Printed in United States

1 2 3 4 5 6 7 8 9

ISBN 1-886679-18-5

Photo Credits:
Paul Berquist 128 (left), 142, 147
    (center), 153
Jeanne Broome 121 (right)
Doris Evans 12, 20, 25, 39, 41, 45,
    46, 47, 59, 63, 66, 68, 69, 72, 73,
    78, 79, 81, 84, 85, 87, 90, 92, 93,
    95, 97, 98, 100, 102, 106, 107,
    108, 111 (top), 113, 116, 121 (top),
    126, 130, 131, 133, 134, 150, 154,
    155, 156, 162, 163, 164
Doug Evans 84
Dede Gilman 104
Merritt Keasey 139
Steven Krasemann 48
Howard Lawler 124
Rico Leffanta 47 (top), 119,
    128 (right)
z. Leszezynski 135
Al Morgan 62, 65, 122
Steve Philllips 33, 37, 51, 52, 57, 60,
    75, 111 (bottom), 120
Carol Polich 129

Illustrations:
Tina Phillips 159–161 (tracks)
Doris Evans 82, 83
Steve Philllips 159–161 (scat)
Deborah Reade 29
Nick Wilson 137

TABLE OF CONTENTS

Qs and Clues: Animals • 109

ACKNOWLEDGEMENTS

Many people took time from their busy schedules to assist me with information, suggestions, corrections, and editing. I wish to extend my sincere appreciation and thanks to following people for their invaluable contributions.

The publication of this book was made possible by the enthusiastic approval of Arizona-Sonora Desert Museum Director, Richard Daley, and the enormous help of Steve Phillips, Publications Manager, who painstakingly edited the text, offered words of advice and encouragement, and saw the project through to completion.

Other Arizona-Sonora Desert Museum staff who offered their expertise are Nancy Laney, Mark Dimmitt, Peter Siminski, Barbara Terkanian, Robert Scarborough, Kimberly Buck, Karen Krebbs, Renée Lizotte, Craig Ivanyi, Sonya Norman, Rich Dulaney, Susan Williams, Carol Madeheim, Robin Kropp, Jacquie Kahn, Kathleen Ryan, and Kathy Moore. Docent Linda Gregonis added welcome input as well. Karen Dunin-Wasowicz and Mary Carbonaro, ASDM volunteers, both took turns copy editing and proofreading the text.

People from various agencies who assisted with trail information were: Steve Anderson and Don Carter, Pima County Parks and Recreation; Meg Quinn, Tucson Botanical Gardens; Karen Bradford and Roger Brian Rutledge, Saguaro National Park Tucson Mountain District (West); Carin Harvey, Saguaro National Park Rincon Mountain District (East); Ainsley Reeder, Oro Valley Parks and Recreation; and Laurel Park, volunteer co-chair of Feliz Paseos Universally Accessible Park.

Thom Hulen, from The Desert Botanical Garden in Phoenix, wrote the Phoenix trails descriptions. His intimate knowledge of the trails in that area was an important and invaluable addition to the trails section.

Carrie Dean, Patricia Dean, and Bonnie Evans helped with editing ideas; Jeffrey Dean supplied me with Hohokam background; Carl Olson answered insect questions; Willie Smith at Jones Photo enlightened me on one-time use cameras.

I extend my gratitude to the Oliveras family, Victor, Erin, Cassandra, and Michael, and the Janice Dungan and her granddaughter, Brooke Srackangast, for allowing me to photograph them enjoying trailside wonders.

A special thanks to my husband, Doug Evans, for editorial and research assistance, for accompanying me on all those trails, and for his love, support and patience while I devoted vacations and weekends to the computer keyboard and mountains of papers and books.

A final note of gratitude to the many children and their parents who asked the questions and inspired me to take on this project.

PREFACE

Learning about nature has been my passion since I was a child. I do not remember what sparked it, but I credit my parents for fanning the flames of interest. They did not have science backgrounds; in fact, they were from the era and background of working-class Milwaukee when children seldom went beyond grade school. But as they got caught up with my excitement as I learned about the world, they became excited and interested as well. When my fourth grade teacher involved the class in a study of birds, mom and dad and I went off to the book store and purchased a set of small bird books. On Saturday mornings we were off to the park with dad's binoculars, leafing through the little books in search of the picture and description that matched the bird on the branch. That set of books with my nine year old notations in the margins sits on my shelf today, along with those old binoculars. Watching tadpoles develop into frogs in a jar on the kitchen counter, pressing leaves in beautiful fall colors, catching fireflies in a jar to watch them flash before releasing them back into the night are but a few of the fond memories of those long ago times.

I chose a teaching career, and the intrigue of the desert brought me to Tucson. A whole new world of cactus and interesting critters awaited. My fourth grade students and I learned all we could from books, then off we went on field trips. Neighborhood walks gave us opportunities to observe birds and plants in yards. We visited nearby city parks and the Arizona-Sonora Desert Museum. What treasured moments to feel the wonder of a child watching a spider spinning a web, a bird feeding young in a nest, or a tiny plant growing from a crack in the sidewalk. Years later I had the privilege of teaching in the little school in Big Bend National Park in west Texas—prime Chihuahuan Desert habitat. There we had an entire national park to use as an extension of our classroom. Geology, paleontology, botany, zoology, even history of the settlers, was tangible. All we had to do was venture out.

Another aspect of my career found me at the Arizona-Sonora Desert Museum. It began as teacher for summer classes. For six weeks each summer my little group of a dozen kids per week and I spent the mornings on the trails making our desert discoveries, and the hot afternoons doing related classroom activities. A few years later I was hired as the Museum's first Curator of Education and for seven years worked with adults and children in many aspects of environmental education. As I developed the docent program and expanded the summer classes, I incorporated the elements of nature study I had learned in the classroom.

My latest job has me on the trails again, this time as the resource teacher for Tucson Unified School District's Cooper Environmental Science

Campus, situated in the Tucson Mountains. There are many aspects to this position including developing environmental education activities and conducting teacher workshops, but my favorite part is the morning interpretive walks with children and their teachers and parents. Each day is a reward. Apprehension about walking a desert trail soon turns to fascination as the children make discoveries along the way.

I never tire of hearing children's questions about natural history. They may be very simple or quite complex and are always interesting. Children are so curious about the natural world and delight in discovering clues they can put together to solve the puzzles that tell us about the world around us.

After an interpretive nature walk a parent often mentions, "That was so informative and fun and the kids really enjoyed learning about nature. I need to take my children on walks like this, but I don't know very much about the desert and I don't know where to find trails that are easy to walk." Thus the idea for this book...a family guide to help parents introduce their children (and grandchildren) to the Sonoran Desert.

Within this book you will find suggestions for leading children on desert walks: simple preparations prior to a walk to ensure a fun, safe, comfortable, and rewarding experience; questions children may have along the trail, and observation clues that will help them answer their questions. Other sections tell where to find easy trails close to town, activities for kids on the walk or back at home, tips for using cameras and binoculars, a glossary of terms, and suggested books for adults and children.

There is a wonderful world waiting out there for your family and you don't have to go far to experience it. The equipment is inexpensive, there is little or no entrance fee, you get in a bit of exercise and fresh air, and your family has a good time learning about nature in general and the Sonoran Desert in particular. You gain another facet to your parent/child relationship and add immeasurably to the storehouse of wonderful memories your children will carry for the rest of their lives.

Doris Evans

Tips and Tricks
for a
Safe and Happy
Adventure

Every adult needs a child to teach.
It's the way adults learn.

—Frank A. Clark

The adventure of a nature walk brings together so many wonderful moments. A brilliantly colored cactus flower, a hawk soaring high overhead, a deer watching you from a hillside are family memories that will last a lifetime. Then there is the good feeling you get after a walk; knowing that you accomplished something quite special. And while you are having fun you are learning important lessons about our environment.

We live in a remarkable place. People come to the Sonoran Desert from around the world to see the cactus, Gila monsters, roadrunners, and desert vistas, yet many of us who live here take our surroundings for granted. We become caught up in urban life and forget about the fascinating natural world only a short distance away. Too often the only view we have of our desert landscape is from the confines of our close-windowed, air-conditioned vehicles.

So, let's break away from that house and car and venture onto the trails. We want the outings to be fun, with a minimum of discomfort, so children will want to go again and again. A little time and thought preparing for our walks will ensure happy hikers.

For families new to nature walks, a desert trail may seem intimidating to parents and children alike. Are we going to get tired? What do we bring with us? What do we wear? What about food? Are we going to have fun?

This section will answer those questions and help you prepare for your outings.

Tips and Tricks for a Happy and Safe Walk

Here are seven tips **before** you adventure on a desert trail. A little planning and preparation ahead of time will go a long way in making your walk pleasant and comfortable.

1. Get in shape

Don't be concerned that getting in shape means following a strict exercise regime. Do not rush out to buy a treadmill! If your family has done little walking, begin with short easy trails so children will think of walking as a pleasant experience. Take some walks in the neighborhood. A stroll around the block, through a city park, or walks to the store or library will help get you in shape. You will notice your muscles strengthen and your endurance improve with each walk. Soon you will be able to walk longer distances and attempt steeper trails. This is a morale builder, too. Your family members will feel good about themselves when they see improvement in their strength and stamina.

2. Wear the right clothing

Proper clothing is important when walking in and exploring the desert. The fun of walking is soon diminished if clothes are not comfortable or appropriate. Sturdy, well-fitting shoes are a must. They need not be hiking boots; good athletic shoes with a gripping —not a smooth—sole are excellent. Avoid wearing brand-new shoes for a hike. To prevent blisters be sure to break them in. Thick cotton-blend socks are good for warm weather walks.

Long pants are recommended, even on a warm day. They will protect legs from scratchy branches, cactus spines, the sun, and scrapes should a stumble occur. Sitting down for a rest or snack is more comfortable when long pants cover and cushion the legs. A lightweight shirt with long sleeves is also a good idea for the same reasons. And don't forget to wear a hat with a brim.

Listen to the weather forecast and dress accordingly.

3. Take only what you need

A small day pack for each child allows them to carry their own food, water, trash, and supplies. It also gives children a sense of responsibility to pack their own gear, and to carry a part of the burden.

Here is a list of items to bring with you. A checklist in the Appendix will help you in your packing.

Food:
Package your food in zip lock bags: they weigh nothing, prevent spills, and take little room in the pack.

- trail mix (gorp) made of a mixture of your favorite cereals, nuts, dried fruits
- cheese, crackers
- peanut butter sandwich
- fruit (apple, banana, grapes, orange)
- carrot or celery sticks
- prepared trail snacks sweetened with honey or fruits
- cookies (oatmeal are good; select cookies that won't melt)

Liquid:
Carry in tightly closing plastic containers. Glass is heavy and WILL break.

- water (a quart or liter for every two miles)
- sport drink or fruit juice (avoid sweet soda, it will only make you thirstier)

Other:
- camera and lots of film
- binoculars
- magnifying glass
- a small mirror (more about this later)
- trash bag
- toilet paper
- sun screen

First Aid:
- comb for removing a cholla stems
- tweezers for removing spines
- bandages
- first aid cream

Optional:
- map
- compass
- notebook and pencils
- field guides

Use a checklist to be sure all essentials have been packed. A sample checklist is in the appendix.

Carry only these essentials; anything else adds weight to the pack. Do not take radios, tape players, video games and the like. Those are out of place on a nature walk. This should be a natural experience — a time to tune into the sights and sounds of the desert. Leave cell phones at home, or use them only for emergencies.

As much as you love your family dog, leave it at home. You will not see as much wildlife if a dog is with you. Many natural areas do not allow dogs anyway, even if leashed.

4. Carry (and drink!) plenty of water

Take enough water and keep sipping it along the way. Even though water is the heaviest item you will tote, it is necessary. Experts recommend a quart or liter per person for every two miles. If you wait until you're thirsty you're already dehydrated. Fruit and sports drinks are good, too, but drink those in addition to water. Avoid soft drinks, they will only make you thirstier.

Take all the water you need for your walk. Do not rely on a water supply along the way. Water faucets are usually not found along the trails. Do not drink from a pond or stream. This water is never safe.

5. Think about the weather

One of the great advantages of living in the desert is that rain seldom interferes with outdoor plans. But the weather isn't always perfect, so you do need to think about sun, heat, and the occasional storm.

Cover exposed skin with sunscreen. SPF of 15 or greater and lip balm with sunscreen will protect the skin from sun damage. Remember the back of the neck, tips of ears, and lips.

In warm weather take your walk early in the morning. The days heat up quickly, and by mid-morning it can be dangerously hot for strenuous walks.

During the summer rainy season it is wise not to be out hiking in the afternoons when storms are more likely to occur—thunderstorms can appear suddenly. If lightning does occur, take shelter near the lowest dry object around; never stand under trees or on high rock formations. If you are on a hill climb down to a lower spot. Avoid being the tallest object. If caught out in the open, squat with your knees tucked under you and only your feet touching the ground. Do not lie flat on the ground.

6. Get the buzz on insects

Even though the desert has a reputation for having lots of bugs, we are seldom bothered by mosquitos, gnats and other buzzing, biting insects. However, there are times when buzzing, biting insects are evident, especially during the summer rainy season. Be careful with bug repellents. Repellents containing DEET can cause health problems, especially in children. If you think insects may be present prepare for them before you leave home. Apply the repellent to clothing, taking care to spray areas of clothing that will not touch the skin. Long sleeves, long pants, hats, and bandanas worn around the neck will also protect against buzzing and bites.

7. Tell the folks back home your plans

Even though you are not going on a dangerous wilderness adventure, it is good practice and a good learning experience for children to let neighbors and friends know of your plans. Later, when your kids are old enough to take hikes without adults, they will remember this important precaution. Tell family, friends, or neighbors:

- where you are going,
- who the members of the group are,
- how long you plan to be gone,
- whom to contact if you don't return,
- what you are wearing and what supplies you have.

Be sure to report your safe return to them, also.

HERE ARE SEVEN TIPS FOR THE TRAIL.

Following these suggestions will help your family enjoy a happy, stress free-walk.

1. Choose Leaders

If your children are beginners in walking trails, have an adult act as leader. If possible, another adult should be at the rear of the line. This will give the children a feeling of security, and they will learn by example about pacing themselves and staying on the trail. As the kids becomes more experienced on the trail, they can take turns as leader. The responsibility will make them feel they have earned your trust and will add to their stamina.

2. Stay on the trail

Staying to the trail is a safety precaution. On the trail you are less likely to encounter cactus spines or scratchy branches and thorns.

Though snakes are seldom encountered, they can easily be seen on the bare ground of a trail. When they are lying on the natural soil or under a plant they are so well camouflaged they are almost invisible. A snake may bite is if it feels threatened by a foot landing close by.

When you walk off the trail there is damage to the natural landscape. Tiny plants are stepped upon and animal burrows are destroyed. When the soil is packed down by footsteps, plants may not be able to grow.

3. Pace yourself

At the beginning of a walk children are excited and want to run ahead, leap from rock to rock, and climb every hill. You don't want to dampen their enthusiasm, but you also don't want them to be exhausted after the first few minutes. Explain that they will get to see it all, and that smart hikers walk slowly. This will allow you to enjoy the surroundings, and the smaller children will not become fatigued. Don't forget to make frequent stops for drinks of water or juice and snacks.

Take breaks along the way. Stop, look, and listen. Children are amazingly perceptive! They spot the small things: spider webs, an insect almost invisible as it clings to the underside of a leaf, a tiny saguaro growing under the cover of another plant, a bite mark on a cactus, a bird nest. It's always surprising to learn about the tremendous variety of organisms that live here. The desert isn't just cactus and coyotes.

4. Bring a friend
Encourage your children to invite friends. It's always fun to share experiences.

5. Offer frequent praise
Praise and positive reinforcement are wonderful encouragement for the child who may be somewhat reluctant to head out on an unknown trail, or who may tire along the way. Comments such as, "What a strong walker you are!" "I'll bet other kids your age would like to get out and walk." "How lucky we are to go on an adventure like this." "I'm proud of you for being such a good naturalist!" encourage kids as they walk along. Also, kids are less likely to complain after they are told what good hikers they are.

6. Build anticipation
The outing will be more meaningful to children if they have helped choose the trail and if they know a little about what adventures may lie ahead. Children love to anticipate adventure. Prior to the walk, talk about where you will go and what you may see. Study a map so children have a sense of where you will be hiking. In which direction from home will you be heading? Which mountain range will you be in or near? Will you be in a national or state park, national forest, or other site? Are there special features to look for along the trail?

7. Have a treat waiting
Keep a simple goody back at the car: ice cold water, a favorite soft drink or snack. If children begin to tire towards the end of the walk, they pick up speed when they know a treat is waiting for them at the end of the trail.

It's Time to Hit the Trail!

Now that you have thought about the details of what to bring and considered the tips for enhancing the outdoor experience for your family, it is time to get out there and enjoy the trails.

Finding the right trails for your family

In a later chapter of this book you will find a list of local trails. We are fortunate to live where natural open spaces are easily accessible, and you may be surprised to discover the number of trails available to the public. Most are free of charge, while others require a nominal fee. You may find a trail near your neighborhood. The brief description of each trail will be helpful in your assessment of which are the most appropriate for the abilities of your family members.

You may wish to try them all. Each offers typical Sonoran Desert habitat, but each is unique, as well—differing microhabitats, vistas, geologic formations, and other wonders make each trail a special experience.

"But, we've been on this trail before!"

Some trails are so close to home, why not make repeat visits? You may think it would be boring to walk on a trail you have traveled before, but did you see it all? There are always new discoveries to make. You might find a plant, a bird nest, or an animal burrow that you walked by before but did not notice. A different time of year will bring out flowers, insects, and birds that were not around during your last walk. Walk the route in the opposite direction and you'll notice new things. Even a different time of day changes the appearance of the trail as the sun shines from another angle.

Actually, repeating walks on one trail is an excellent way to learn intimate details about desert life. You become aware of changes, both subtle and dramatic. You become attuned to life histories of plants and animals as you observe them over a period of time.

For many years my husband and I repeatedly walked the same desert trail for exercise as well as to enjoy the sights along the way. We were constantly making new discoveries and learning new things about past discoveries.

We watched birds build nests in the cactus and bushes next to the trail. Our bird books told us how many days until the eggs would hatch, and we were delighted when we heard the hatchlings peep from within the nest as the parents carried in food. We saw the chicks grow, leave the nest, and call noisily from nearby branches still asking to be fed.

We became acquainted with the habits of different species of birds. Some nested in the same spots year after year: a dove nested in the crook of a saguaro arm, a pair of kestrels fed their young in a former woodpecker cavity in a saguaro, a cactus wren built a nest within the same jumping cholla. We knew just where to look for a male hummingbird. He perched on a high branch of the same tree. From there he launched off to perform his acrobatic flight to impress a nearby female. Each spring we watched the cycle of life continue.

It was interesting to notice the habitat choices of different kinds of birds. We could count on seeing sparrows in the underbrush, woodpeckers clinging to the sides of saguaros, cactus wrens standing on spiny chollas, and hawks and kestrels perched on tall saguaros or utility poles. Along one part of the trail is a grassy baseball field. There we knew we would find killdeer, grackles, and starlings poking for insects in the grass.

We chanced to see a screech owl peering from a cavity nest in a saguaro. Each time we passed that saguaro we would look up to see if the owl was there. Some days it was, other times it was either somewhere else or snoozing within the cavity.

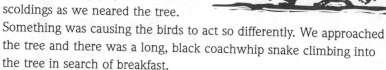

A certain palo verde tree was a favorite perch for a group of cactus wrens. One morning we heard loud scoldings as we neared the tree. Something was causing the birds to act so differently. We approached the tree and there was a long, black coachwhip snake climbing into the tree in search of breakfast.

On any one walk we would see only a few species of birds, but over time, we totaled over 80 species, all from the same trail!

Birds are easily seen, so many of our observations were bird related, but there were many other discoveries to make as well.

We watched changes in a large packrat den. At times we knew it was inhabited because pieces of fresh cactus and other new debris littered the roof of the den. At other times it was abandoned. Nothing new was added and it began to collapse. Did a coyote have a packrat meal? When would another packrat move in?

We spotted a neat, round hole alongside the trail. Reflected light from our little mirror revealed the hairy legs of a tarantula before it scooted deeper into the burrow. With each walk we noted the burrow, some days we caught glimpses of the spider, other days not. In fall the hole seemed to disappear, but careful examination revealed that the tarantula had covered the entrance to wait out the winter months within its burrow. The next spring we glanced at the entrance site each time we passed by, and one day the burrow was reopened. Our spider friend was back in business, waiting for insect prey to come along. We watched this process for over ten years. At our last check, the tarantula was still there.

After repeated sightings we knew where a herd of javelina was likely to be resting in a wash and where a jackrabbit sat in the shade of a tree. As we became familiar with the animals we thought of them as old friends and talked about "our owl," "our tarantula," and "our kestrels." The desert creatures became so personal to us. We cared about them.

We never knew quite what to expect when the spring annuals sprouted and bloomed. Depending upon the winter rainfall and temperature patterns, different flowers dominated the landscape each year. One year there was a carpet of purple lupine, the next year yellow composites (daisy-like flowers) were everywhere. It was always a surprise.

Early one July morning we saw what we thought was a large white tissue within a creosotebush. Upon closer inspection we discovered a breath-taking sight. We were looking at the flower of a night-blooming cereus. Hidden within the bush was the rest of the cactus — thin, dark gray-green stems blended in with the branches of the creosote bush. The cereus is related to the saguaro and as is typical with that group of cactuses, the blooms last for only one night. But the interesting thing about the night-blooming cereus is that all the cereus within an area will bloom the same night! We had walked within inches of this cactus for years and never knew it existed until it bloomed. With time we found many more cereus. Sometimes we were lucky to find the dead-looking stems within another bush, but mostly we found them by looking for the spectacular flowers. Each summer we watched the buds develop and tried to predict the night the flowers would open and perfume the air.

We never tired of our walks on that same old path. Had we walked the trail only once or twice we would never have had so many sightings, so many experiences, and learned so much — and we only needed a short walk to reach it. No, we did not live in a remote area. All these wonderful natural events were taking place within the city limits of Tucson in a patch of desert surrounded by busy streets!

Nature will bear the closest inspection.
She invites us to lay our eye level with
her smallest leaf, and take an insect view
of its plain.

— Henry David Thoreau

Respecting the Environment

There is nothing in which the birds differ
more from man than the way in which
they can build and yet leave a landscape
as it was before.

— Robert Lynd

ow that you've learned what to bring along, and how to keep the kids enthused about their adventures, let's add to your quality time by gently interjecting outdoor ethics. When children learn the rules early, the rules stay with them for a lifetime. This, too, is another morale booster. Having strong outdoor ethics binds the family together and makes everyone feel good about doing the right thing.

Actions

A family outing provides a good opportunity to develop outdoor manners. Learn and follow the rules of the area. Children become attuned to the good habits of not littering (if you pack it in, pack it out), staying on trails and not taking shortcuts, not picking flowers or collecting anything that is against the rules of the area. The National Park Service's adage, "Take only pictures; leave only footprints" is a wise one to incorporate into your family's hiking ethic.

Children love to throw rocks, but the trail is not the place. Rocks may be shelter for animals and removing them disturbs their homes. Throwing rocks may injure plants or other hikers who may be walking below you on a hillside and not visible from your trail. Rocks fascinate kids and they should be encouraged to pick them up and examine them, but then the rocks should be placed back where they were found.

Respect all animals. Observe spider webs without breaking them. Examine holes and burrows, but do not toss pebbles or kick dirt into them. Enjoy watching nesting birds from a distance, but do not get so close that you disturb them.

A small mirror is a wonderful tool to reflect sunlight into a burrow, or to point out something of interest off the trail, but use it with caution. If you want to point out a lizard on a rock or a bird on a nest, aim the light near the animal, not on it.

Trail etiquette is important. Children must learn to stay far enough behind the person ahead of them to avoid stepping on heels. Although talking about the experiences is important, keep voices low so that you can hear desert sounds. Be polite to others on the trail by passing them on the right. Public lands are the home to plants and animals. They also belong to everyone, and we all have a responsibility to treat the land with respect.

"I gotta go to the bathroom!" Be prepared for this familiar lament. The availability of toilet facilities is listed on each of the trail descriptions in the trails chapter. Most have pit or flush toilets near the trailhead and it's always a good idea to give a "last bathroom call" to the group before heading out. However, it's always a good idea to be prepared for an emergency when you are on a trail that is longer and not crowded. Carry a small roll of toilet paper and zip lock bag. When an emergency potty stop is necessary, the person in need should leave the trail and walk about 200 yards away. The used toilet paper is placed in the zip lock bag to be disposed of later. Toilet paper is litter, too, and should not be tossed on the ground. If you are on a longer, back country trail, a serious potty stop may be needed, in other words, a bowel movement. For these walks, take along a small garden trowel. Again, leave the trail and walk about 200 yards away, dig a small hole, deposit waste in the hole and cover it up. Again, the used toilet paper should be sealed in the zip lock for later disposal.

Attitudes

Parents' attitudes are most important. If you show interest and excitement about the walk and the discoveries made, children will echo this enthusiasm. Afterward, looking up information about something you saw, or identifying a plant or animal in a field guide, not only makes the walk more meaningful but it also promotes the fun of research.

Even though snakes and spiders may not be your favorite creatures, try not to exhibit fear or loathing when you see one. Refrain from terms such as "bad," "ugly," or "nasty." They create fear and prejudices in children about plants and animals that are difficult to overcome. Instead, talk about your observations. What are the characteristics of the plant or animal? How might they be important in feeding, defense, or camouflage? In doing some research you may learn what interrelationships it has with other organisms and its importance in the web of life. What you or your kids may have considered unattractive at first may turn out to be fascinating.

Be aware of misinterpretations. There is a great deal of oft-repeated faulty information out there about nature, and about desert life in particular. If you are not sure of a fact, it's best not to express it until you and your children check it out later. It's difficult to unlearn an erroneous idea.

There are also many misconceptions and misunderstandings about the workings of nature. One of these is predation. Predators have usually been portrayed as the bad guys in stories. However, predators play an important role in controlling populations of their prey. Animals are not "mean," "scary," or "bad" because they prey upon other animals. All animals need to eat. (Remember, humans are predators, too.) It's also a good idea to use the word "predator" in place of "enemy." The coyote is not the enemy of the rabbit. "Enemy" implies hatred and hostility. There is no hate involved when the coyote catches a rabbit; the coyote is hungry and the rabbit is a meal. The word "enemy" connotates negative feelings.

It is difficult to avoid anthropomorphism—giving animals human attributes. We are always tempted to interpret the actions of animals in human terms, and it does give us an empathy for animals. After all, many folk tales and fables do just this. But also keep in mind that our interpretations may be giving us false impressions of what the animals are doing. The antics of a roadrunner may give us a chuckle, the owl may look wise with its big eyes, the coyote may seem wily as it disappears into the desert, and the snake may appear sneaky as it slithers beneath the brush. But after we have made our observations, discuss with the children how they think the actions and appearances are helping the animals carry out their lives. Are they hunting, hiding, or perhaps defending their territories? The family can have fun brainstorming interpretations. Animal behavior is a fascinating study.

How often do we hear the desert described as a "harsh environment"? It may seem harsh to us when temperatures soar, but to the countless species of plants and animals that live here, it is not harsh at all. They are adapted to desert conditions, or they wouldn't thrive here. Just as the whale is at home in the ocean depths and the polar bear is at home on the Arctic ice, desert plants and animals are well suited to life in this hot, dry environment.

Please do not feel daunted by this list of do's and don'ts. As you explore and observe, these concepts will soon become an integral part of your family's interpretations of our fascinating desert world.

Qs and Clues: Helping Children Interpret Nature

Tell me, I may forget;
show me, then I may remember;
but involve me, and I'll understand.

—Chinese Proverb

s your family walks along the trails, enjoying the beauty of the surroundings and the exhilaration of exercise and fresh air, children will notice plants, animals or signs of animals, and even rocks that will capture their attention and prompt questions. "What is it?" or "I wonder what's happening here?" The kids will also have many hypothetical questions. "What if we see a dangerous animal?" "If we find a horny toad or tortoise, can we take it home?" Children are superb observers. They will see things along the trail that adults would walk by and not notice, and they will have questions — lots of questions!

And here is the heart of this book. In this chapter are a variety of questions kids are apt to ask along a desert trail, as well as ideas to help you help your children develop sensory awareness and thinking skills as they explore for answers.

Do not feel pressured to make a lesson out of everything you see. The pure enjoyment of seeing a mountain vista or a tiny flower at your feet are moments to savor without words. But the trail offers unlimited opportunities to expand upon our children's understanding of the world and to develop those critical thinking skills, so valuable in life. It is okay not to know the answers or the names for things; the experiences are what count. What children learn from direct exposure to nature are far more valuable than learning names. However, we humans are label conscious, so look up the bird you saw, or the plant that interested you; identify it, read about it, and add that information to your notebook, journal, or scrapbook. It is easy to remember the name of something when you have observed it, researched it, and jotted down your findings.

What's Going on Here?

Along the trail encourage your children to discover and figure things out for themselves. Everything they see has a story. Look at the parts of the story and ask them to put those parts together to come up with the whole story. These need not be complicated. Here's an example:

The parts of the story:
- small hoof tracks in the soil
- a few long, stiff, gray and black hairs on the ground
- signs of digging at the base of a plant
- exposed roots that look as if they've been chewed
- scat (animal droppings) containing plant material

The whole story:
- Javelinas came by (recently if the tracks are still clear), rooted around in the soil with their hooves or noses and dug up and ate the roots.

Develop sensory awareness. Rub or scratch and sniff leaves. How do they smell? Does the smell remind you of anything? Feel the textures of plants, of rocks. Look at colors, shapes, sizes. Compare— what are the similarities and the differences? Listen to the sounds of birds, of wind, of insects or lizards moving about in the underbrush. We don't want children to fear the desert, but caution is always wise. Observe a snake, but keep a safe distance. There are some things to touch, but others are best seen without touching.

Okay, now you and your family are ready to hit the trails. What will you see? What will you learn? What adventures await you? There are so many life forms, seen and unseen, along the trail. And be aware of the geology, too. So many stories will unfold, if you only stop, look, listen, and think about the clues around you. In this section you will explore the things you are most likely to discover along a typical Sonoran Desert trail.

Each "story" is covered in the following format:

- A question or comment your child may say.
- How to search for clues that may answer the question or expand on the comment.
- Information to help parents put the clues together to come up with the story.

The parents' information section is for you to use at your discretion. Use as much or as little as you wish, depending upon your child's age and interest level. This is written at a 4th to 5th grade level so the information can easily be transferred to children.

Whenever feasible, the immediate answer is given at the beginning of the parents' information section to give you a feel for the information that follows. But please refrain from giving children a pat or immediate answer. They learn best if they figure things out themselves. Not every question will have a precise answer. Scientists do not know everything, thus there are many unanswered questions. Rather than be frustrated, you may use these situations as part of your children's education. Your family can have fun speculating on the why, what, and how of questions. It's important for kids to understand not everything has been learned. Maybe they will be the ones to make discoveries one day.

A very wise, old adage says it best:

I hear and I forget.
I see and I remember.
I do and I understand.

As children search for answers to their questions help them become aware of:

- Similarities and differences and what they tell us
- Patterns of life
- Interrelationships between living things and their surroundings
- Adaptations to desert conditions

The subjects of the questions or comments are arranged by categories (geology, plants, reptiles, and so forth), however one subject seldom stands alone. For every observation that you make you discover other aspects of the environment are involved as well. That, too is an important lesson. Seeing and learning how one organism affects another provides your family with graphic illustrations of the web of interrelationships in nature.

Qs and Clues: the Desert

Why is this a desert?

The clues to the answers to this question cannot be found by using the sensory clues used in the other questions. Instead maps and diagrams help us to understand the causes of deserts and why they are where they are.

To answer this question many factors come into play. The answer to the younger child would be quite simplified. "Deserts are places where there is little rain. We do not get much rain here because the rain falls in other places before it can reach us. Little rain means the plants and animals that live here must be able to live without much water."

To the older child, perhaps nine years old on up, searching for answers to this question involves looking at maps and thinking about physical properties of air. When these components are tied together children are able to grasp the concepts of what makes a desert.

Why is this a desert? There are various conditions that cause a place to be desert, but they all have to do with the physical location of that place on planet Earth which, in turn, affects the weather patterns. The distance of a place from the equator, the distance from oceans, and location of nearby mountain ranges are some of the factors that create desert environments.

Here are the factors that have created the Sonoran Desert.

Rain Shadow

- When moist air is blown in from the sea and is pushed up and over mountain ranges, there is less pressure exerted on it in the

Cool Fact!

Temperature differences between night and day are greater in deserts than in any other place. Dry air and clear skies allow maximum solar heating during the day and the temperature rises. At night the dry air and clear skies cause the opposite effect: the day's heat radiates back into the sky and the temperature drops quickly. There is often a 30° F (16° C) difference between the day's high and the night's low temperatures, and the difference can be as much as 50° F (28° C)!

28

higher altitudes. This causes the air to expand and cool. Cooler air cannot hold as much moisture as warmer air, so the moisture falls as rain on the upslope or windward side of the mountains. This is what happens in parts of the Sonoran Desert. By the time the air has crossed mountain ranges in California and Baja California, Mexico, the moisture has been "squeezed" out of it. Those of us who live in Sonoran Desert areas of Arizona and Sonora live in a rain shadow. This shadow isn't blocking the sun, it blocks the rain. Our land remains dry.

High Pressure

- The earth's equator receives the most direct rays of sun, therefore it is always hot. Hot air rises because it is lighter. It rises high

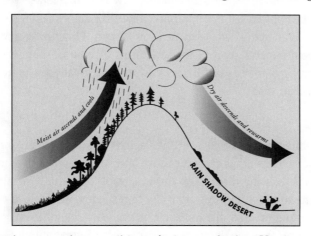

into the atmosphere until it can't rise any further. Up there it spreads out to the north and south and cools at those high altitudes. Cool air is heavier than warm air, because it is denser, and so it descends. This sinking air falls at about 30 degrees latitude at either side of the equator. The Sonoran Desert is about 30 degrees north. This continually descending air means we have a pile up of air above us. As the air presses down it heats up because pressure creates heat. Hot air can hold more moisture than cool air, so any moisture within this warm air is not released as rain. Our land remains dry.

If this is a desert, why does it rain?

As in the previous question, "Why is this a desert?" immediate clues are not available. But you can think about our rains. When do they usually occur? In what ways are winter rains different from summer rains? Using the information you learned in the desert question will help you answer this question, too.

In many parts of the Sonoran Desert there are two rainy seasons —summer rains and winter rains. In the Tucson area the rainfall is divided about evenly between these two. In an average year about six inches of rain fall in winter and about six inches fall in summer for a total of about twelve inches annual rain. Phoenix averages about eight inches, and Yuma only three. Of course, there is seldom an average year and rainfall amounts can vary greatly season to season and year to year.

Winter Rains

Our winter storms begin over the Pacific Ocean. These are large weather systems that carry moisture from the ocean as they move eastward over the mountains and valleys of California. The air contains so much moisture that the rain shadow effect does not cause it to drop all of the moisture on the west side of the mountains. When it reaches the desert areas it still holds a great amount of water and we are treated to welcome winter rain. Our heaviest winter rains are from storms that push far south and then turn north, thus doing an end run around the highest coast and peninsula mountain ranges. Our winter storms give us low, gray clouds that may cover most of the Sonoran Desert area and may remain for several days. The gentle soaking rains may continue for a day or more.

Summer Rains

July and August bring our most dramatic weather. Temperatures soar to 105°F (40.5°C), perhaps to 110°F (43°C) and more. After many weeks of high temperatures heating the land, conditions are right for the summer rains to begin. Our first clues are the fluffy white clouds that appear in midday. Watch for changes in those clouds. You will see one or more quickly growing until half the sky is filled with a huge billowing cloud. Bolts of lightning flash here and there within the darker folds. The top of the cloud flattens to an anvil shape, so high up that this part of the cloud is made of ice crystals. Strong winds carry dust and sand ahead of the rain as downdrafts from the storm cloud hit the ground and spread out. The rain comes suddenly, huge drops fall hard and fast. If you are caught out in the storm the raindrops sting your skin. Blinding flashes of lightning are followed by ear-splitting claps of thunder. Within ten or twenty minutes perhaps an inch or more of rain has fallen before the storm moves on across the desert. The sun reappears and a brilliant rainbow, often a double one, arches across the sky. The rain has come down so quickly there is no time for much water to soak into the soil. Sheets of water stream down hillsides and fill the washes or arroyos, creating instant rivers. Unlike the widespread winter rains, these

> The term monsoon comes from an Arabic word for seasonal wind. In the Sonoran Desert moving air brings rain in winter as well as summer. But we are more aware of the strong summer winds that bring the spectacular storms, that is why we think of the summer rains as monsoonal. But monsoon refers to the wind, not the rain. There is debate among scientists as whether our winds are truly monsoons or not.

Cool Fact!

storms are local. A downpour may drench your yard but your friend's yard a block away may not receive a drop of rain.

Some call these summer storms , but this is an incorrect use of the word. Monsoon is derived from an Arabic word meaning seasonal wind. The storms begin over the waters of the Pacific Ocean and the Gulf of California. Wind carries moisture-laden air from the sea and swirls it around, bringing it to the Sonoran Desert as southeast winds. The summer heat causes columns of humid air to rise high into the atmosphere. There the air cools and moisture condenses, changing in form from a gas to drops of water, even snow and hail in the higher reaches of the thundercloud.

Summer storms are more likely to occur in the middle to eastern part of the Sonoran Desert. The western part, along the Arizona/California border usually does not experience the summer storms because the moisture has been dropped from the clouds over higher-elevation lands before reaching areas along the Colorado River. So if you live in the Tucson-Phoenix area you are treated to the summer storms. If you live in the Yuma area your summers are usually dry.

Another type of summer storm are the *chubascos* (Spanish for squall or sudden shower). These are tropical hurricanes of September and October which follow the monsoon season. These storms begin off the west coast of Mexico south of Baja California. The storms move northwest and follow the Pacific coast of Baja until westerly winds turn them inland. They cross over the Baja California peninsula and move up the Gulf of California picking up moisture and energy from the warm sea. The chubasco hits land at the upper Gulf, around Yuma, and may deliver as much as six inches of rain on a desert that averages three inches of yearly rainfall. These storms do not occur every year, but when they do develop they drench the driest part of the Sonoran Desert.

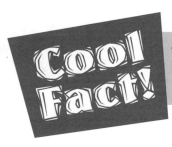

The Spanish term for the summer rainy seasons is *las aguas* which means "the waters." The winter rainy season is called *equipatas* which means "little packages."

Who poured cement on the ground?

As you walk along a trail you may see areas that look as if someone dumped concrete on the ground. Examine this "cement." Is this the work of careless people or is it a natural part of the desert? Do you see other rocks cemented into the concrete? Can you find rocks that look as if someone poured whitish gray concrete over them?

No, no one dumped their extra concrete onto the ground. This is a natural rock formation common in deserts. It may look as if it were recently poured, but it took thousands of years to form.

This natural cement is called caliche (kuh LEE chee). It is calcium carbonate that was formed by ancient rains. As rain falls it gathers acid from the atmosphere. The rainwater mixes with the soil and dissolves minerals in the soil as it seeps downward into the ground. The mixture dries and hardens into a hardpan layer buried beneath the soil surface. Wherever we see caliche at the surface, it is because the surrounding soils and rocks have eroded away.

Caliche is found in deserts because there is not enough rainfall to dissolve and wash the caliche particles to underground water reservoirs. Caliche is not found in climates where there is more rainfall. Like limestone, it is composed of calcium carbonate, a mineral which fizzes when an acid such as vinegar is dropped on it. (Try putting a drop of vinegar on caliche next time you have a chance. It's fun to see it fizz!)

Cool Fact!

Why does the desert have all those empty spaces?

As you walk along the desert flats, you see many empty spaces between the bushes. Take a close look at a bare spot next to the trail. Get down close to the ground in a place where people have not walked. Examine it. How are the rocks placed on the surface? Does it look as if it's a big gazillion piece jigsaw puzzle? Can you see a grayish-greenish crust the soil in places? Take out your hand lens and examine the crust. What do you see?

I f you have lived or traveled in parts of the country where it is cooler and wetter, there is much more plant life covering the ground. In fact you may not even be able to see the ground in those green places. The desert looks very different. Even though many places in the desert may look empty, there is really quite a bit going on in those "empty spaces."

One of these is the desert pavement. Find a flat, open area that is covered with small stones. You will notice that they fit together like a jigsaw puzzle. This neatly layed out rock cover is called desert pavement. Scientists believe this is caused by our cycles of rain and drought. Wet soil swells, lifting larger rocks to the surface. When the soil dries, it shrinks, forming cracks into which the tinier grains of soil and smaller rocks fall. Each time the soil becomes wet and then dries out this process continues. As the smaller grains of soil move downward, the larger rocks are moved to the top. This natural pavement forms a protective cover over the soil and helps prevent

Cool Fact!

Here is an example of how long-lasting disturbance to desert pavement can be. Prehistoric people "drew" large figures of animals, humans, and designs on the desert floor by moving the dark varnished rocks of the desert pavement to expose the lighter underlying soil. These can still be seen, especially from an airplane. These figures, called intaglios, were made over one thousand years ago!

34

erosion. When the wind whips across the desert you will notice dust flying from a road or trail, but not from the natural areas where the rocky desert pavement covers the finer soil. Native plants are able to grow through this rocky layer, but non-native plants usually cannot. You will find tumbleweed and other non-native plants only in disturbed areas, such as roadsides and once-plowed vacant lots.

Another part of the desert floor that can be damaged if you step on it is the cryptobiotic soil. "Crypto" means camouflaged or hidden. "Biotic" has to do with living things. So "cryptobiotic" means "living things that are hard to see." Look carefully along the soil surface. If you see a dark, greenish-gray crusty coating over the ground, you are seeing a community of living things. Cyanobacteria (blue-green algae), algae, fungi, lichens, mosses, nematode worms, and microarthropods are some of the organisms found in cryptobiotic soil.

This crusty mass may not look impressive, but it is very important. This collection of organisms aid desert life in many ways. They are the first colonizers on barren soil surfaces. They add nitrogen to the soil, absorb rainwater, glue together soil particles, and form a protective covering over the soil. All of this helps other, larger plants to grow, plus it helps prevent erosion. These colonies are tiny ecosystems, complete with producers, consumers, herbivores, and carnivores. Notice the difference in appearance in the soil after a rain. The cryptobiotic colonies change from being dry and soil-colored to a velvety green.

This covering of tiny organisms survives under the desert sun and hard rains, but it cannot survive if it is trampled under the soles of our shoes. After you have examined a patch of cryptobiotic soil with your hand lens, continue on the trail without disturbing the fragile "skin" of the desert floor, allowing the little organisms to carry on their important jobs.

Why are there so many different kinds of rocks? Why are they different colors?

Isn't it fun to sit down on the ground and take time to look at the rocks? You may not think much about the rocks that cover the ground — aren't they just hard brown things? But because you are learning to observe and discover, you have found another interesting feature in our desert: the rocks. Test your observational skills. How many colors can you see? Do some rocks sparkle in the sunlight? Can you find veins, or stripes of color through a rock? Shapes are interesting, too. Do the rocks have sharp or rounded edges? Use your hand lens to get a close-up view.

Children are fascinated with rocks. Small children, especially, love to sift through them looking for the "prettiest" rock...one that sparkles or has an interesting color or shape. This is best done in a wash or arroyo where pebbles and small rocks abound and no harm is done by scattering a few stones. For the younger child, playing with the rocks is satisfying in itself. They may sort them according to size, color, or shape. They may feel textures and look at tiny crystals through a magnifying lens. Taking time to do these activities develops sensory awareness and alerts children to the fact that rocks can be fascinating and so different from one another. They become involved with one more interesting outdoor experience.

It would be so convenient if there were easy explanations for childrens' questions about rocks. Unfortunately, full answers can be very involved and require considerable prior knowledge of geologic processes and chemistry. But you want to encourage your child's interest in geology and there are many aspects of the subject you can discuss.

Rocks are made of minerals. Minerals have many colors, depending upon the materials they are made of. The colors you see are in the minerals that make up the rock. There are many, many kinds of minerals. You probably have heard the names of some: quartz, galena, turquoise, mica, and calcite are a few. The next time you are at a museum that has a geology exhibit look at the display of minerals. What beautiful colors and shapes they are! Many times we can't identify a rock by its color. Rhyolite for example, can be any color.

There are three major rock types on earth: sedimentary, igneous, and metamorphic. They are classified by how they were formed.

Igneous rock is formed when molten material, melted by tremendous temperatures within the earth, cooled and solidified. Children will think of lava pouring from volcanoes as an example of igneous rock, and that is one type. But not all molten rock breaks through the earth's crust. Molten material may push into underground rocks, cool, and harden without reaching the surface.

The sparkles you see in rocks may be caused by minerals that crystallized as the molten rock cooled and hardened. Igneous rock often contains crystals. If the molten (melted) rock cooled very slowly while still underground, it will have crystals large enough to see. Melted rock that came to the surface by way of a volcano or vent cooled quickly and will have fewer visible crystals, or none at all.

Sedimentary rock was formed from bits and pieces of other materials which were often washed down a river, then cemented together. They can be formed in different ways. Old rocks are reduced to particles through the actions of water, freezing, heat, dissolving acids, and breakage as other rocks tumble down upon

them. These small pieces are carried by water or wind which deposit them someplace else. Eventually these bits and pieces are cemented together to form rock. Rocks that look and feel as if sand had been glued together is probably sandstone.

Another kind of sedimentary rock is made up of pieces of shell, coral, and other organisms that once lived in ancient seas. When these animals died, they dropped to the ocean floor. Their hard parts remained. Some were broken, some remained whole. The bits and pieces eventually cemented together. The old seas receded, and today we see the results of this process as a type of limestone. You may discover fragments of fossil sea creatures in an outcrop of limestone rock. Sedimentary rocks are the only kind of rock that can contain fossils. Non-living materials, too, may be deposited on the floor of a sea or lake which later form a solid rock mass. One example is another kind of limestone made up of a mineral called calcite.

Metamorphic rock is rock that was once sedimentary or igneous. Extreme pressure or temperature deep underground recrystallized the material and a new kind of rock was formed. Examples of metamorphic rock are quartzite, slate, schist, and gneiss.

It may be tempting to take a rock home, but remember rocks are an important part of our environment and should be left where they were found. Also, removing rocks from areas such as national parks or county parks is illegal. If your family would like to start a collection of rocks be sure you remove them only from places where it is legal to do so and you have the landowner's consent.

Who spray painted those rocks?

At first glance it indeed looks as if someone spray painted some of the rocks bright green, blue-green, orange, gray, black, or yellow. Use your magnifying lens for a close look. Is it paint or is it something else? On which side of the rock do you see the color — the shady or sunny side? Gently touch the colored part. Does it feel different than the rest of the rock? How many colors can you find?

What you are looking at is a living organism called lichen (LIE kin). It is actually made up of two organisms living together in a relationship called mutualism which means that each organism needs the other and cannot live on its own.

One organism is a fungus. The other is an alga. The fungus uses the food produced by the alga part, because fungi cannot make their own food. The algae may need the fungi for moisture, minerals, and something to hang on to. It is the fungus part that you see. The layer of alga is below the surface. There are many species of lichen, and different species produce different colors.

Did you notice that the lichens you see are usually on the shady side of rocks or on shady cliffs in an arroyo? This tells us that it's too hot and dry for lichens in areas that get full sunshine, especially in summer. But they grow very well in places that are usually shady.

Lichens grow all over the world, not only in deserts. They come in many colors. Some look like paint, others look crusty, and some look like little bushes. They are often found on rocks, but they may grow on the soil surface, on tree trunks, and even on buildings.

Here is a pronunciation guide for you:

singular: alga (AL ga)   singular: fungus (FUN gus)
plural: algae (AL jee)   plural: fungi (FUN jie)

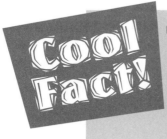

Lichens are important in a number of ways:
- They're the first organisms to grow on rocks and probably help break down the rock to form soil.
- Some animals eat them (especially in the Arctic).
- Some are used to dye material different colors.
- They are very sensitive to polluted air. Dying lichens are indicators of pollution.

Did someone burn (or varnish) the rocks?

You may find rocks that look dark and shiny as if they were covered with varnish. If the coating is very dark it may look as if the rock has been burned. Pick up the rock, but remember how it had been positioned on the ground. Do you find that one side of a rock is coated with a darker color than the rest of the rock? Which side has the darker color? The side that was exposed to the light, or the side stuck into the soil? Feel the dark part. Does it feel different from the lighter sides?

I f you thought the rocks were varnished, you were right in a way. This dark coating is actually called desert varnish. The varnish can be shades of black, orange, or brown. It probably took thousands of years for the varnish to coat a rock.

How did it get there? Materials floating in the air, such as bacteria and clay, and minerals such as manganese and iron, settle on the rock surfaces. The bacteria slowly oxidize and concentrate these minerals, cementing them to the rock surface while absorbing

A prehistoric petroglyph chipped through desert varnish

41

additional airborne and waterborne matter. Over thousands of years a shiny, smooth dark-colored layer of desert varnish builds up and coats the part of the rock that is exposed to the air.

If you are hiking in an area where you can see cliffs, look for dark streaks where water poured over the rocky sides. This is a related varnish composed of mineral and decayed vegetable matter.

Desert varnish forms only in the driest, hottest parts of deserts. Though we do not understand the details of its formation, somehow bacteria that live on the rock surfaces deposit the minerals on those surfaces.

Some prehistoric people chipped their designs on rock surfaces covered with desert varnish. When the dark color was chipped away, the lighter rock underneath showed through. Pictures chipped into rock surfaces are called petroglyphs.

I like walking in the wash (arroyo)!
It's different down there.

Walking in a wash, or arroyo, presents a different view of the desert. What do you notice in and along the sides of the wash that you may not see on a higher trail? Are the plants taller, larger leafed, and greener? Perhaps you see more signs of animals. Look for nests, scat, footprints, and burrows on the cliffsides. What factors would cause the differences in habitat between the wash and the higher ground?

A wash or arroyo (Spanish for wash) is a dry river bed. Desert trails often take you into a wash for at least part of the route. As you leave the higher trail and drop into the wash you find yourself in quite a different habitat. With each bend of the wash there seems to be another surprise ahead. There are so many different things to observe.

Look at the plants along the wash and compare them with those along the higher trail. Notice that the palo verdes, mesquites, and jojobas are much larger. Leafier and greener plants grow in the wash, too. Along the sides of the wash the plants grow close to one another, not spaced apart as above.

These differences are caused by water. But, it doesn't rain only in the arroyos. Why would there be more water in the wash? Look up at the hills that surround you. What happens to the rainwater after a heavy rain, especially a summer storm. The rain falls so fast and hard that not all of the water can soak into the ground where it lands. Therefore it flows down the hillsides to the lowest places — the washes. Here water collects and flows down the wash. A dry river bed can become a raging river in a matter of minutes. A huge volume of water tumbles through the wash and some of it soaks into the sandy or pebbly wash bottom. Palo verdes, mesquites, and jojobas, small and shrubby above, grow large and green in the wash. Catclaw acacias and desert brooms are examples of plants that are scarce above, but abundant along the banks of a wash.

43

After many, many years of water flowing through the arroyo during summer rains, the rocks and soil on the sides wear away in a process called erosion. As you walk along the wash you see that the sides of the arroyo may be very high or shaded by large trees. Look at the north facing banks where sunlight seldom reaches. Here you will see mosses, ferns, lichens, and sellaginella — plants that can grow only in the cooler, moister, shady microhabitats that washes provide.

Cool Fact!

Bedrock mortars can be found along some streambeds. These are round, smooth depressions in the rock made by ancient desert inhabitants as they ground seeds and other material by pounding them with stone pestles. If you come across mortars, sit down next to one. Pretend it is hundreds or even a thousand years ago and you are grinding mesquite beans to make flour for bread. What would life have been like for the desert people who lived here 600 to 800 years ago? Look at the scene around you and imagine how it might have looked different then and how it may have remained the same.

The sides of arroyos are also good places to observe the roots of plants. Roots normally are hidden underground, but along wash banks the soil erodes (wears away) with each rainfall, exposing long roots. Isn't it amazing how far they reach out as they slowly grow through the hard soil and cracks within the rocks? Find a root and try to trace its path to its parent plant, perhaps on the cliffside high above your head.

When flowers bloom in spring and summer you will see different flowers in the wetter, sandier wash bottoms than in the higher ground.

In what ways do arroyos make good animal habitats? You will see burrows of all sizes dug into the gravel cliffs. Who may have made the holes? Coyotes, foxes, badgers, squirrels, and packrats are some of the animals that find this a good place to dig shelters. Lizards, snakes, scorpions, centipedes, spiders, desert tortoises, and insects also move into these cool, protected places. If the day is hot, the temperature within a deep burrow will by many degrees cooler than the outside air, and quite comfortable for the animals as they wait for the cool of the evening.

You may see jumbles of rocks scattered about. Over many years of rain storms and the powerful flow of water, large rocks tumble down the wash and pile up on one another. These, too, provide good places for animals to rest, protected from heat and predators.

You may come upon a rocky canyon. Look for depressions in the rock where water would collect after a rainfall. These are called tanks or, in Spanish, *tinajas*. What a good place for thirsty animals to come for a drink!

Deer and javelina spend the hot days beneath the large trees and along the north facing sides of the arroyo. In these shady refuges the temperature is many degrees cooler. Larger trees also mean many places for birds to make their nests. Arroyos provide good nesting and resting habitats.

In the center of the arroyo few plants grow. If a seed germinates and a small plant begins to grow, it washes away when water rushes through. The wash makes a natural pathway for the trail and for the animals, as well. In fact, washes are important routes for many animals. These are called wildlife corridors.

Washes are safe to walk most of the time because there is little rain in the desert. But if rain is predicted, especially during the summer rainy season, it is wise to use caution and move to higher ground. Even though it is not raining where you are, there may be an enormous rainstorm upstream, a few miles away. The water cascades down the hillsides, collects in the arroyos and within minutes the water rushes down. Where there was dry sand a few minutes before, may now be a deep and dangerous river. But that's a fascinating part of the desert climate — the extremes. One minute the land is dry and parched, then a rainstorm erupts. Rivers gush. Lakes appear in the flat lands. The rain stops, rivers subside, lakes evaporate. The clouds disappear and the sun dries the land again.

What is the Arizona state bird (flower or tree)?

On almost every Arizona desert trail you are likely to see real life examples of some Arizona state symbols. Look at the desert trees. Which one is the state tree? Listen for the state bird. The state flower may not be blooming, but you can find the plant that produces it.

Three living symbols you are most likely to see are:

State Bird: Cactus Wren

Arizona's state bird is the largest member of the wren family. Look for a bird about 8.5 inches (22 cm) long with a dark reddish-brown cap, a broad white streak above each eye, brown and white streaked back, and a spotted breast. It is often seen perching on a cactus or tree branch. Its call is a harsh *cha cha cha* that sounds like an old car trying to start up on a cold morning. The cactus wren was officially designated Arizona's state bird by legislative action on March 16, 1931. (No, the roadrunner is NOT Arizona's state bird. New Mexico claims the roadrunner for that distinction.)

State Flower: Saguaro Blossom

The large, white waxy-petaled flower of the saguaro cactus is Arizona's state flower. You may see saguaros bloom as early as April but they are at their peak in May and June (though an odd flower can appear any month of the year). The flowers open at night and close during the following day. On sunny hot days they close in early morning. On cooler, cloudier days they may stay open until mid-day. Once a flower closes it will not open again. The saguaro blossom was adopted as the floral emblem of the Arizona Territory on March 8, 1901, and officially confirmed as the state flower on March 16, 1931.

State Tree: Palo Verde

The palo verde is the state tree, officially adopted in 1954. In Arizona there are two native species of palo verdes plus an introduced species and some hybrids. The two natives, the foothill and the blue palo verdes, share the honor of state tree. Palo verde is Spanish for green stick, an appropriate name for this common Sonoran Desert tree. If you spot a tree with a green trunk and green branches and twigs, you are looking at a palo verde.

Other official Arizona state symbols:

State Mammal: Ringtail

The state mammal is the ringtail. Though the ringtail lives in the Sonoran Desert, this nocturnal mammal is seldom seen. Its habitat is usually canyons with available moisture, rocky outcrops, and caves. It is the size of a large squirrel. Distinguishing features are a pointy nose, large black eyes, and a long fluffy tail ringed with black and white. It is sometimes called a ringtail cat, but it is not a cat at all. It is a member of the raccoon family.

State Reptile: Ridge-nosed rattlesnake

The state reptile is the Arizona ridge-nosed rattlesnake. It lives in the cool canyons and pines in the higher elevations of the Huachuca, Patagonia, and Santa Rita mountains in southeastern Arizona. It is one of four rattlesnake species on the list of threatened and endangered native wildlife in Arizona. Habitat destruction and reptile collectors are threatening the species.

State Amphibian: Arizona Treefrog

The state amphibian is the Arizona treefrog, one of two native treefrogs found in Arizona. The range of the Arizona treefrog is confined to the oak, pine, and fir forests in the mountains of central Arizona and western New Mexico along the Mogollon Rim and in the Huachuca Mountains in Cochise County.

State Fish: Apache Trout

The state fish is the Apache trout. The habitat of these fish is high elevation, small streams. They once occupied the headwaters of the Salt, San Francisco, and Little Colorado rivers. Today they are distributed in five streams on the Fort Apache Indian Reservation and in Apache-Sitgreaves National Forest in the White Mountains. Their numbers are increasing thanks to conservation efforts by various agencies.

Other state symbols:

State Fossil: Petrified Wood

The Arizona state fossil is petrified wood. The largest known accumulation of petrified wood in the world is in Petrified Forest National Park in northern Arizona. Most of the fossilized wood in the Park is of an extinct species of tree that grew 225 million years ago, during the era of the early dinosaurs. The scientific name of the species is *Araucarioxylon arizonicum.* It doesn't have a common name. Its relatives still growing today are primitive conifers (evergreen trees). These conifers are native to the southern hemisphere, but some have been introduced in the United States. If you see a monkey puzzle tree you are looking at a species somewhat similar to the tree that became Arizona's state fossil.

State Gem: Turquoise

The state gem is turquoise. The blue-green glossy stone has been used in southwest Indian jewelry for centuries. It was approved as the state gemstone in 1974.

State Neckwear: Bola Tie

The state neckwear is the bola tie, which consists of a cord with a decorative piece attached to a sliding clasp. A chunk of turquoise mounted on the clasp and silver-tipped cord ends is considered the official style, but bolas are commonly adorned with polished petrified wood, Indian-made silver jewelry, or any material with a southwestern design.

Why do we have to stay on the trail?
Why can't we take a shortcut through that open place?

You have been walking on the trail for awhile and are ready to go back to the car. Why not shortcut across the desert? What could it hurt? Look at the area you are thinking of cutting across. What would you be stepping on? Do you see tiny green plants beginning to grow? Do you see holes in the ground where kangaroo rats, squirrels, spiders, or insects have built a home?

E'ven though some places look empty, there are many things that can be destroyed if you leave the trail. Two things that can be damaged are the desert pavement and the cryptobiotic soil. See the entry **Why does the desert have all those empty spaces?** to learn about their importance.

But these aren't the only things that can be damaged if you leave the trail.

If it has rained recently, little plants are pushing up through the soil. The seeds may have laid on the soil for years and are now starting to grow because the rains have finally fallen at the right time. Stepping on the young plants will kill them.

Cool Fact!

Trails on hillsides usually wind back and forth. They were made that way for good reasons. The walk is a little longer, but you will be less tired than if you go straight up or down a steep hill. Winding trails prevent erosion. If the path is straight up and down, water flows right down the trail, making a deep cut. Have you seen stones or logs imbedded in certain places along a trail? The trail crew built these to direct water runoff so that will not do damage. Some people are impatient (plus extremely inconsiderate) and cut down the hillside from one section of the trail to another. This opens the way for erosion damage when the runoff from rain pours down the vertical scars.

50

Many desert animals make their homes below the surface of the soil. Stepping on a hole may cause it to collapse and cover up the entrance to a burrow. See the entry Are those snake holes? for more information on the animals that live in those burrows.

Whenever you stray from the trail, damage is done. Footprints often remain. People who come after you see those footprints and may follow them, thinking it is another trail. Soon there is a mark on the land that will last for years.

Other good reasons for staying on the trail are for your safety. You are more likely to trip over branch or rock, or encounter cactus spines if you are off the trail. Also, if a rattlesnake is near, you will see it on the bare ground of the trail. A snake lying on the natural soil or under a shady plant is so well camouflaged it is almost impossible to see. A snake that feels threatened by a foot landing close by could strike in self defense.

You can see so much from the trail without having to walk on natural desert floor. Always be a responsible hiker and help to preserve our precious desert landscape.

Can I take home a rock or part of a cactus skeleton?

There are so many interesting rocks and woody cholla or saguaro cactus "skeletons." It is tempting to take home souvenirs of your walk. Carefully pick up a rock or piece of wood. Do you see signs of a plant or animal living beneath the object you picked up? Do you see tiny insects or their burrows? Do you see webbing material made by insects or spiders? Perhaps small plants are beginning life. Carefully replace the rock or wood exactly as you found it. Is it a good idea to remove these things from the desert floor?

There are countless rocks and pieces of dead plants scattered about. It seems it wouldn't hurt to take a few home, but it is best to leave everything as it is. Most rocks and pieces of wood provide needed shade or shelter for tiny plants and animals. By taking any of these you are removing the "roofs" of their homes. Also, rocks, sticks, and other debris on the desert floor retain moisture which is utilized by tiny life forms living in these microhabitats.

Taking anything disrupts the habitat of plants and animals. One little rock may not seem important, but if everyone who walked by decided to take something, soon there wouldn't be much protection left for the little creatures, nor much to see for those who pass by this way. These pieces of the desert floor are of much more value left in place in the natural environment than in your house.

Because of these problems of removing things from the wild, it is against the law to take away natural and cultural objects from public lands such as national, state, and county parks and from private land without permission of the owners.

Instead of taking objects, there are other things you can do that make even better souvenirs. Take pictures, make sketches or water color paintings, or take time to look closely at an interesting rock or stick or cactus skeleton and observe it in its natural place. What better memories you will have than by taking it home, stuffing it away in a drawer, and soon forgetting about it.

When we try to pick out anything by itself, we find it hitched to everything else in the Universe.

— John Muir
My First Summer in the Sierra

Qs and Clues: Plants

What's that dead, mossy stuff covering the ground?

You come upon dead-looking moss-like plants covering the ground. Feel them. Use your hand lens for a closer look. If it hasn't rained recently they feel dry and hard and appear to be dead. Look at your surroundings. Where are these plants located? Are they on a hillside? Are they on the side of a wash? Which direction is the hill or wash facing? Does the sun shine here much of the day?

You are looking at selaginella (sel a ji NEL a). It belongs to a group of plants called spike moss. Notice the cover of scalelike leaves along the stems.

In dry times the selaginella is gray-brown, its leaves are pressed against the stem, the branches are curled, and the plant appears to be dead, but it is not dead at all. This is how it looks during times of drought when it is dormant, or inactive. But what a change occurs when it rains! As the roots absorb the water, the leaves and stems plump out and within a few hours the plants are bright green. Now it can carry on its life processes of food production and reproduction. As long as the soil is moist, selaganella forms a soft, plush, green carpet covering the ground. When the rains stop and the soil dries, it becomes brown and dormant again.

Did you notice that selaginella occurs in places where the sun does not shine directly? It grows on north-facing hillsides and cliffsides or sometimes under the growth of other plants. It cannot tolerate long periods of full sunlight.

Remember the trails where you see selaginella. Next time it rains, either summer or winter, return to see the selaginella in its green glory. It is hard to imagine you are looking at the same plant that looked so dead before.

Can we drink from a barrel cactus if we get lost?

You have probably heard stories about people lost in the desert who survived by cutting open a cactus, usually a barrel cactus, and drinking the juice inside. Examine a barrel cactus, or any other large cactus. Imagine you are lost and thirsty. How would you get inside the plant? Look at those sturdy spines. Look at the tough skin beneath the spines. Do you think you would find a cool, clear supply of water inside?

After a close examination of a barrel cactus, you realize some of the problems you would encounter if you attempted to extract moisture from it.

Problem #1:
Getting to the pulp is very difficult. The work of cutting into the tough, spiny covering is likely to cause a great deal of water loss from sweating. Yes, a machete would work, but if one had thought to bring a machete along, one surely would have thought to carry enough water.

Problem #2:
The water in the pulp is tightly bound in the gooey tissues, somewhat like a damp sponge; not much liquid could be squeezed out.

Problem #3:
The raw pulp of many cactuses is not edible. Chollas and prickly pears may have toxic levels of oxalic acid; other cactus contain bitter alkaloids; some barrels contain

57

substances which cause diarrhea, or may cause you to vomit — the last thing a thirsty person needs! The pulp has a bad taste and may make you even thirstier.

The tales about lost hikers surviving by drinking from a cactus when they ran out of water are just stories. These stories are unfortunate, because they may give a false sense of security to desert hikers who think they can find a ready water supply if they drink all the water they carried.

Even though cactus would not be a water source for us, native desert peoples have survived on the moisture contained within barrel cactus in emergency situations, but not without problems such as diarrhea and joint pain. People who live off of the land have more intimate knowledge and experience than city dwellers.

Look! I found a fern fossil!

It's fun to look at all the interesting rocks along the trail. Sometimes you find a rock that has a dark fernlike pattern. Look closely using your magnifying glass. Is it a real fossil, or is it something else?

It is exciting to make new discoveries along a trail, and a real fossil would be quite a find, but the fernlike design you find occurring in rocks is not a fossil at all. Fossils are the remains or imprints, preserved in rocks, of plants or animals that lived in pre-historic times. Fern fossils are very rare in the Sonoran Desert area.

These pretty fern or tree-like patterns are called dendrites. (Words that begin with "dendri" or "dendro" have something to do with trees.) A dendrite is formed when mineral-laden water slowly seeps along open cracks in the rock. A film of iron or manganese is slowly deposited, forming a dendritic pattern.

Although this is not a real fossil, the dendrite you found is interesting, too. Admire your find, then place your rock back on the ground as you found it.

Dendrites can be found in many kinds of rocks and minerals, including agates. Maybe you have seen jewelry with little "fern forests" imbedded in clear quartz.

59

Why are bugs crawling around in that flower?

If there are flowers, there will be insects in and around them. Peek into the flowers. How many different kinds of insects do you see? What are they doing? Do they have yellow dust on their bodies? Put your finger on the yellow powdery parts inside the flower. Does some of it stick to your fingers? Use your hand lens to examine the flower parts. You will also discover more tiny insects within the flower. What's going on here?

The insects are gathering food in the form of sweet liquid nectar or powdery pollen.

Many flowers are brightly colored and have an odor, usually a sweet, perfume smell. The color and odor attract insects as well as hummingbirds and other creatures. Treats await the visitors. The flower produces a sweet nectar, pooled at the bottom of the flower cup. The powdery yellow pollen is perched atop the many stamens.

Inside the flower, the insect sips the sweet nectar or gathers the pollen. As it does this, some of the dusty pollen sticks to the insect. Many insects have hair-like bristles covering their bodies and the pollen easily sticks to these hairs. When the insect has eaten it flies to another flower. Some of the pollen the insect carried rubs off on the pistil of the other flower. The pistil is the large structure protruding from the center of the flower. If the pollen is from the same species of plant the flower will be pollinated. That means the pollen that landed on the pistil will cause a tube to grow down the length of the pistil carrying the pollen grain to the ovary in the base of the flower, fertilizing the flower. When this happens the flower begins to form a fruit and inside that fruit are seeds. Without insects (or birds and other animals that visit flowers) many flowers could not be fertilized, seeds would not form, and there would be no new plants.

As you examine the flowers along the trail, notice the many colors and shapes. Peek inside the flowers and find the stamens and pistils. Some flowers have lines on the petals which are "lane markers" for insects. They are called nectar guides. In the insects' eyes these lines stand out and guide them deep into the flower to the pollen.

Here is a demonstration of the flower-insect connection that children like to do. You should be close by to be sure your children stay clear of spines. Wiggle a finger among the stamens in a prickly pear cactus. (The stamens are the thread-like stalks tipped with nobs of powdery pollen.) Remove the finger and notice the stamens move! They close in towards the center of the flower. The finger acts as an insect crawling about. The stamens close around (but do not trap) the insect, ensuring lots of pollen will stick to its body as it crawls out.

Insects may enter flowers for other reasons besides feeding on pollen or nectar. Some eat the flowers, consuming petals and the reproductive parts; others use flowers for shelter.

Some birds are also pollinators. When a hummingbird sips nectar from flowers, the pollen rubs off on its bill as well as the feathers around the bill. The bird pollinates the flowers as it travels from plant to plant.

Without insects, birds, and other flower visitors doing the pollination work, most of the plants we know and rely on for food would not exist. As you peer into a flower and watch the busy insects, think of the important contribution they make in our lives.

Other plants, such as grasses, are wind-pollinated. Gusts of wind carry millions of pollen grains into the air. Some land on the right species of plant and pollination occurs.

Are all the spiny plants cactuses?

Examine the different plants that have spines or other prickly things.

Look at some of the plants you know to be in the cactus family: saguaros, prickly pears, chollas. Study the way the spines grow from the plant. If flowers are blooming, study the structure of the flowers. Notice the thick, waxy petals and the mass of pollen-tipped stamens.

Find plants that have woody branches with sharp thorns. How do the thorns grow on the branches? If flowers are blooming, notice their structures.

How are these plants alike? How are they different?

Plants with spines, thorns, or other kinds of prickles are not all cactuses. The easiest way to determine whether a plant is a cactus or not is to look at the spines and note how they grow on the plant.

The skins of cactus plants have little round spots called areoles. The spines always grow from these spots and usually grow in clusters or groups, though with some species the spines are single.

Find a bush or tree-like plant with woody thorns. Those thorns are usually not in groups. They grow one by one along the stems, and no areoles are present. This is not a cactus. You may be

ocotillo

looking at one of the plants in the bean family: a mesquite or an acacia.

Find a plant with long, whiplike woody stems branching from the ground. Examine the stems and you will find rows of sturdy thorns spiraling around the length of the stem. Many people think this is a cactus, but the single thorns and absence of areoles tell us it is not. It is in a family of its own, the ocotillo family.

Here are some of the clues that tell us a plant is a cactus.

Flowers

A cactus flower has many sepals (those are the green leaf-like structures around the outside of the flower base), many petals, and many stamens.

Stems

Stems are thick and fleshy. This adaptive feature allows storage of moisture in the form of a thick, milky substance which is not lost from the plant as easily as water. Stems swell when moisture is stored and contract when moisture is lost. Most cactuses have cylindrical stems (saguaro, cholla, and hedgehog to name a few), but some stems are flattened (prickly pear). Larger cactuses develop woody, supportive skeletons. The skin is thick and waxy which slows evaporation of stored moisture. The stems contain the green chlorophyll which is necessary for photosynthesis (food manufacture) to take place.

Leaves

Most cactuses have no leaves. Exceptions are the new growth of chollas and prickly pears which have small fleshy leaves which soon drop. There are cactuses that have leaves but they live in more tropical climates.

Spines

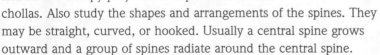

Cactus spines grow in clusters and emerge from roundish pads called areoles. (Flowers and stem buds also emerge from these pads.) Look at different kinds of cactuses and notice the different arrangements of spine clusters. They grow on the surfaces and edges of prickly pear stems, along the outer pleats of barrels, hedgehogs and saguaros, and on the bumpy projections of pincushions and chollas. Also study the shapes and arrangements of the spines. They may be straight, curved, or hooked. Usually a central spine grows outward and a group of spines radiate around the central spine.

Glochids

Glochids are tiny hair-like spines that surround the larger spines on prickly pears and chollas. They easily detach when they become stuck in skin or clothing.

63

Is that one of those cactuses that jump on you?

You may have heard people tell tales of cactus jumping out at them. Can cactus, or any plant, actually jump? There *is* a cactus called "jumping cholla." It is one of the most common of the cholla cactuses in the Sonoran Desert. Find one and get up close to it (but don't touch it). Hold your hand up close to a branch. Does it jump on you? Examine the spines. Can you see tiny hooks at the tips? Look beneath the cholla. Do you see stem pieces laying on the ground?

The cholla (CHOY ah) did not jump on your hand because plants cannot jump. But it's easy to understand how this cactus got its reputation. Here's what actually happens. You walk by a cholla and unknowingly brush against a stem. Some of the tiny sharp hooks at the tip of each spine attach to your skin or clothing. As you move away the stem breaks from the plant and is now stuck on you! Also, be aware of cholla stems that have fallen to the ground or you will discover them attached to your shoes.

If you get impaled by cholla (and it will happen sooner or later if you hike in the desert) here are some hints on what to do:

- Do not panic and wave your arms around. If the piece is stuck on your arm this will only drive the spines in deeper.

- Do not reach for it. Your hand will then be stuck and you'll be in deeper trouble.

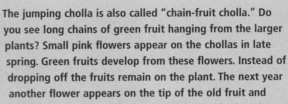

The jumping cholla is also called "chain-fruit cholla." Do you see long chains of green fruit hanging from the larger plants? Small pink flowers appear on the chollas in late spring. Green fruits develop from these flowers. Instead of dropping off the fruits remain on the plant. The next year another flower appears on the tip of the old fruit and another fruit develops. This causes the long chains. The jumping cholla is rather unusual this way. Most plants drop their fruits each year.

QS AND CLUES / PLANTS

- Here is where your comb becomes a perfect cholla-removing tool. With the tines inserted between skin and cholla, a quick flicking motion will extricate it with only momentary pain. Be sure no one is standing in the line of fire or you will have another cholla-impaled victim to tend to.

- Chances are that all the spines will have been pulled out. If some remain, use tweezers to remove them.

Did you see cholla joints littering the ground beneath the cactus? Because the pieces detach so easily, a strong wind, rain, or hail storm will knock many stems from the plant. It may seem strange that a plant would lose its parts so easily, but this is one of the ways this plant reproduces. When a piece lands on the ground it may take root and grow into a new cholla plant. Coyotes, javelinas, and deer are some of the animals that scatter cholla stems. Stems are caught in the fur and later drop to the ground.

Another cholla that easily loses its stems is the teddy bear cholla. This cactus looks somewhat like the jumping cholla, but it is smaller, denser, and the spines are so silvery that the plant looks like a soft teddybear. But do not be fooled. Don't pet this teddy bear!

There are other cholla species that are not as densely spined and do not easily lose stems. Do you see other kinds of cholla plants? Look for cactus with jointed, sausage-shaped, spiny stems.

Why do I smell rain?

You walk by a shrub with small, yellowish-green, shiny leaves. Your nose picks up a familiar aroma. The air smells the way it does when it rains. Stop at the shrub. Cup your hands around the end of a leafy branch. (Don't worry, there are no spines or thorns.) Blow on the leaves, then take a deep sniff. It smells like rain! Examine the leaves. Notice how they shine and sparkle in the sunlight. Feel them. Do they feel slightly sticky or greasy?

You have come upon the plant that makes the desert smell like rain. It's called creosote bush or greasewood. In Spanish its name is *hediondilla* which means "little stinker."

Creosote bush grows in all of our North American deserts, even in the driest, hottest places, such as Death Valley. Its leaves wear a protective coat. That sticky, greasy leaf coat you feel is resin, a natural substance produced by some plants. It prevents the moisture inside the plant from escaping into the air. The resin gives the creosote bush its odor. Other desert plants may drop their leaves in dry weather, but the creosote bush leaves stay on. They may get yellow and dusty, but unless they suffer an extreme drought, the leaves do

not fall. The next time it rains take a deep whiff of the desert air and remember the creosote bush.

After a rainfall, no matter what time of year, little yellow flowers appear on the bush. Insects visit the flowers, spread the pollen, and seeds are produced. Now you find little cotton balls where the flowers had been. These contain the seeds. A few weeks after the appearance of the cotton balls, the seeds have matured and the fuzzy balls open up. If you can find the seed balls in this stage, use your lens to get a close look. You will see that each ball separates into five sections, and each section contains a seed. If the seeds have not yet opened, take one cotton ball and gently pull it apart. You will see five seeds nestled within.

The creosote bush is believed to be the oldest living plant in the world. Individual stems live a mere 100 years or so, but new stems grow from the outer edges of the root mass, forming a ring around the decayed central stems. That ring of stems eventually dies, and new growth continues at the edges of the ring. Century after century the ring of creosote bushes expand and may form separate bushes, but they are descended from a common seed and are clones of the original plant. By studying the growth rates of certain large creosote bush rings in the Mohave Desert, scientists have estimated that the original central stems were growing over 11,000 years ago!

The creosote bush is not eaten by many animals—the resin may not taste very good. Jackrabbits are about the only mammal to eat creosote bush leaves, and they do so only during severe droughts when leaves from other plants have died. However the creosote bush is important to animal life for other reasons besides food. Rodents dig burrows in the shady soil beneath the plants. Snakes, lizards, spiders, and other animals make use of these burrows. More than 60 insects feed from the flowers and foliage of the creosote bush or use the stems as places to lay eggs.

Can you find a small green or brown ball attached to a branch? Look at the question, **What are those balls on the creosote bush?** to find out what it is.

Which plants are good to eat?

Imagine you are a Hohokam (HO-ho-kahm), a native American who lived here in prehistoric times, or a member of a pioneering family living here before there were grocery stores. Food came from the land. Of course animals were hunted for meat, but plants are a very important source of food, too. Look around. Which plants do you think would provide food? Would it be easy to collect and prepare enough edible plant material for your survival?

Cactus fruit is probably the first food that comes to mind. You may have eaten the fruit of the prickly pear in jam or syrup. You have seen pictures of the Tohono O'odham gathering saguaro fruit with long poles and may have tasted the sweet juice of the saguaro fruit. Even today many people enjoy gathering and preparing wild foods.

But as you look at the dry, scratchy plants of the desert, you may wonder what else could be eaten besides cactus fruit. Surprisingly there is a great deal of food to be found in desert plants.

Here are a few examples:

Fruit
The sweet, juicy pulp of the saguaro and prickly pear cactus fruit is cooked to make a jam, jelly, or syrup. These fruits appear on the cactuses in summer.

The yellow fruits of the barrel cactus appear in fall. They are sour and not as juicy as prickly pear or saguaro fruits, but they can be eaten raw.

The small round red fruits of wolfberry and hackberry can be eaten raw.

Seeds

The acorn-like seeds of the jobjoba can be eaten, but they are bitter and have never been a major food source for desert peoples. The seeds are filled with a liquid wax which can make you ill if too many are eaten.

The seeds of wild gourds (buffalo gourds and coyote melons) are dried and eaten.

Sunflowers, grasses, and many plants you may think of as weeds produce nutritious seeds which are ground into flour.

Seed pods

The seed pods of members of the bean family (mesquite, palo verde, ironwood) can be ground into flour and used in bread and muffins.

Flower buds

The unopened flowers of the cholla are baked and used in salads and stews. Removing the tiny spines, however, is a tricky process.

Greens

The leaves from many plants that appear after spring and summer rains are used in salads or cooked as vegetables.

The new pads that form on prickly pear cactus are cooked and diced and used in a variety of salads. The Spanish name for prickly pear is *nopal*, and the diced, cooked pads are called *nopalitos*. You can find these in jars, already prepared, at the grocery store.

Flowers

The flowers of ocotillo, yucca, and other plants can be eaten.

Roots

The root bulb of wild onions can be eaten raw or cooked.

Research has shown that native plants provide nutritious foods, help prevent diseases, and keep the body functioning properly.

But after saying all this, should you begin picking and eating things from desert plants? The wise thing is NOT to eat from wild plants unless you have an expert with you to tell you what is safe to eat. Many plants look similar to one another; one may be good to eat, the other may not, and could make you ill. Then there are the problems of allergic reactions or a bad taste that lingers.

Also, think of the ethics of picking off parts of plants. Damaging plants or picking off plant parts spoils the experience of those who come after. It's best to leave these foods for the animals who depend on them. For these reasons it is against the law to remove plant parts in national parks and many other public places.

There are local organizations that offer classes and trips where you can safely and legally enjoy a desert harvest. See pages 213–214 for their names and addresses.

Where are all the flowers?

You have seen the beautiful photographs in magazines: fields of yellow, white, red, orange, and purple flowers carpeting the desert floor. Examine the ground along the trail. Do you see any little green plants pushing up through the soil? What time of year is it? If it is spring, were there winter rains, or was it a dry winter season? If it is fall, was there a lot of summer rain, or was it fairly dry?

The photos of pretty flowers are usually taken in late winter or spring after a good winter rainy season. There are flowers after a summer rainy season, too, but are not as spectacular as the spring wildflowers. They tend to be taller, more weedy-looking, and include many grasses.

The orange, yellow, and purple carpets of flowers you may be thinking of are the "escapers." Many of them are annuals, plants that live less than a year. You may not see any seeds on the ground, but they are there, tiny and perhaps covered by a dusting of soil. IF the rains begin in late fall, and IF they continue through the winter at a rate of about an inch per month, and IF the temperatures are not too cold or too warm, THEN there may be one of those beautiful flower shows that bring out all the photographers. But most winters do not produce just the right combination of factors and few spring wildflowers appear. You may be disappointed, but it is no problem for the plants. The seeds continue to lie on the ground, perhaps for many years. Then there is a winter where all the right conditions are met and ZOWIE, little green sprouts push through the soil and for a

Did you ever wonder how the spring and summer flowers "know" when to bloom? The temperature as well as the rainfall must fall within certain limits to trigger the seeds from annuals to germinate or the underground roots of perennials to send up stems. Thus spring flowers will not apper in summer and summer flowers will not grow in spring.

few glorious weeks in spring the desert is a wonderland of color. When that happens, enjoy! You may not experience this again for many years.

Do spring flowers ever grow after summer rains? Do summer flowers grow after winter rains? The answer is "no." How do they "know" when to bloom? The seeds of winter/spring and summer annuals respond to temperature and day length that causes them to germinate at the right time of year. If a winter annual were fooled into germinating by a summer rain, it would quickly die in the high temperatures of summer days, and a summer annual would not do well in cool spring conditions.

owl-clover

pygmy white daisy

globe mallow

What's that plant with the big leaves (or nuts)?

A shrub catches your attention because its large, thick, oval leaves look quite different compared to other desert plants. Touch the leaves. How do they feel compared to the leaves of other nearby plants? Make a scratch in one leaf with your fingernail and notice what happens at your scratch mark. Use your magnifying glass to take a close look. Do you see the shiny coating and the tiny white hairs that grow on the leaf surface? Now look at how the leaves are positioned along the branches. Imagine the summer sun high in the sky. Which part of the leaf would receive the most intense sunlight? Which part would be shaded? Hold out your hand so that your palm receives the full force of the sun. Now turn your hand sideways so only the edge of your hand is aimed towards the sun. Do you feel a difference in temperature?

Perhaps it was the plant's large nut-like seeds that caught your attention. In late spring green, acorn-looking nuts droop from the branches of some of the plants. These turn brown during the summer, then disappear as they are eaten by animals.

This plant is the jojoba (ho HO bah). You noticed it because its thick, larger leaves and densely leafed branches give it a different look compared with the other plants which have smaller, more feathery leaves or no leaves at all.

If you learned how small leaves prevent a plant from losing too much water, you may

wonder how this plant can survive with all those big leaves. When you scratched the leaf surface did you notice the scraped area is moist and darker green? When you felt the leaves, examined them under the magnifying lens, and compared them with leaves of other desert plants you noticed the jojoba leaves are thicker and wax-coated. That is one way the jojoba is able to survive under the hot desert sun. The waxy coating holds moisture within the leaf. Under a magnifying glass you can see tiny white hairs growing on the surface of the leaf. These help reflect sunlight. Also, the leaves are a grayish-green rather than a dark green. The lighter color reflects sunlight, just as lighter colored clothing keeps us cooler in summer.

Notice how the leaves grow from the branch. Rather than lying flat-side up, where the mid-day sun would heat the entire leaf surface, they are at an up and down angle. The sun hits the edges of the leaf, therefore there is less water loss.

The nut-like seeds develop in spring and in early summer; they are shiny green and easy to see. As they mature they turn brown. Deer and many rodents eat them. You may not see any in winter and early spring, but look at the ground beneath the plants and you may see the brown seed husks littered about.

You see nuts on only some of the plants; those are the females. Jojobas do not have male and female parts in one flower as do many plants. The male flowers are on one plant and the female flowers are on another. The wind blows the pollen from the male flowers. Pollen that lands on the female flowers cause the seeds to form. One way to remember this is females have the kids, and the nut-like seeds are the beginnings of baby plants.

You can tell male and female plants most any time of year. If you see small stalks holding a bunch of tiny gray-green leafy clusters, that is the male plant. If you see a small stalk holding a single bell-like structure, that is the female plant. The flowers are greenish and small so unless you look closely you don't notice them. If you walk among jojobas in spring examine them. The male flowers are full of yellow pollen. Flick your finger at the flower and a cloud of yellow pollen bursts into the air.

The wax contained in jojoba seeds is used commercially. Medicines, cosmetics, and machinery lubricants are some of the products made with jojoba seed wax. Read the labels on shampoo and lotion at home or at the grocery store. Can you find any that say, "Made with jojoba oil"?

74

Look at the big nest in the tree!

You see a large, roundish mass of twigs within the branches of a tree. It looks like a bird's nest, but is it? Find one of these masses nearer to the ground so you can get up close to examine it. Does it look like a nest now? Or does it look like something growing on the tree? Look into the mass of stems. Can you see where it's attached to the branches of the tree? In fall and early winter you may see tiny red fruits growing from the twigs. After your careful observations you realize this is not a nest at all; it is a plant growing right out of the branches of a tree.

This is mistletoe. The roots of most plants grow in the ground, but the root-like structures of the mistletoe (they are not true roots) grow into the tree.

The fruit of the desert mistletoe is red and ripens in fall and winter. This is an important food source for many birds, especially the phainopepla. Look around for a bird with black, shiny feathers, red eyes, and a cardinal-like crest of feathers on its head. That's the phainopepla. It eats insects, too, but when the mistletoe fruits are ripe the phainopeplas gather to feed. You will see them perched near

clumps of mistletoe. Desert mistletoe berries are edible to humans, but those of the leafy "Christmas" mistletoe are poisonous.

If you find a plant with red fruits, pick one and squish it between your fingers. Do you see the seed stuck to your finger? Shake your hand and look again. Is the seed still there? The seeds are very sticky. After a bird has been eating the fruit it may rub its bill on a branch, leaving a seed stuck to it. Or, seeds pass through a bird's digestive system and when they are deposited on a branch they stick to it. When conditions are right a seed will germinate and the plant will grow, sending its root-like structures into the tree.

The tree is the host and the mistletoe the parasite. The "roots" of the mistletoe grow into the host tree and take some moisture and nutrients from the host. But the mistletoe contains green chlorophyll which allows it to produce its own food. Therefore it is a partial parasite. It needs its host plant for some nutrients, but can also produce its own food.

Cool Fact!

Mistletoe is an important part of our desert landscape and has been around for a long, long time. The population of mistletoe and desert trees remains the same, so there is no danger of our trees being killed off by mistletoe. You may see dead trees covered with dead mistletoe clumps, but perhaps those trees were very old and therefore more vulnerable to the rooting of mistletoe seeds and then weakened by the overabundance of mistletoe plants growing on their branches.

Many species of mistletoe grow around the world and in many climates. The one you see in the desert is called desert mistletoe or mesquite mistletoe. Notice the tiny scalelike leaves. The mistletoe used at Christmas time is a different species. It has larger leaves and white fruits and lives in higher, cooler elevations.

How can plants live in the desert?
Does anyone water them?

It's hard to believe that plants can grow in a place that can be so hot and so dry for so long. The desert covers a vast area; do you think it would be possible for people to water all the plants? Not only is it not possible, it is not necessary. Desert plants can live a long time without water. Let's look for clues on how this works.

Search for plants that have these characteristics:
- waxy coatings on the leaves or stems
- tiny leaves
- no leaves at all
- large stems where water may be stored
- light colored or fuzzy leaves
- light gray spines covering a cactus

What do these clues tell us about how plants are able to live in the desert?

Desert plants can be placed in three general categories of water conservation strategies.

The water hoarders
The water hoarders store water within plant tissues.

- The large, rounded stems of cactuses store volumes of water, and the waxy outer surface reduces water loss.

night-blooming cereus

- The roots of many desert plants spread far outward, allowing the roots to take in water from a large area. The water is then stored within the plant. (Example: The roots of a saguaro reach out in all directions, like spokes of a wheel. The roots may be as long as the saguaro is tall.)
- The root may be a large, water storing turnip-like tuber, such as the night-blooming cereus.

The drought tolerators

The drought tolerators are able to tough out long periods of no rain.

- The lack of water-losing leaves conserves moisture. Cactus plants are good examples of drought tolerators as well as water-hoarders.

- Many desert plants have small leaves. Smaller leaf surface means little water is lost from the plant into the dry air.

- Mesquite trees have very long tap roots which may reach underground water tables.

- The waxy coating on leaves reduces moisture loss. Creosote bushes and jojobas are examples.

- The edges of leaves are turned upward and do not receive the full force of sunlight on their surfaces. Look at the leaves on the jojoba bushes and notice their orientation in relation to the sky.

- Fine, gray, downy-covered leaves and stems reflect the sun's heat. The silvery gray leaves of the brittlebush are covered with a "hairy" coat.

- Some species of cactus are covered with whitish spines which reflect heat and shade the plant. Look for the small pincushion cactus; the spines form a cover so dense that you cannot see the green skin.

The avoiders and escapers

The avoiders and escapers do just that: they avoid or escape dry, hot seasons.

- Many trees, shrubs, and small perennials drop their leaves during dry times. Ocotillos are well known for this, but palo verdes and other desert trees and shrubs also shed leaves during drought conditions.

- Plants can't run away from unfavorable conditions; instead some escape by dying. But they leave something very important: their seeds. Plants you may not see at all are the "escapers." These are the small flowering plants you see after a rainy winter or rainy summer. The seeds lie in the soil, sometimes for many years. When rainfall and temperatures are just right the seeds germinate or begin to grow. The plants

grow quickly. They produce flowers, followed by seeds, and then they die. The seeds fall to the ground and may lie there for years until conditions are just right for them to germinate. Plants that live for less than a year are called annuals.

• Some species of plants exist for years as underground roots or bulbs. When conditions are right they send up stems which leaf out and flower. Members of the lily family such as the mariposa lily and wild onion are examples of perennial escapers. Perennials are plants that live more than a year.

Spring annuals could not survive the summer heat, and summer annuals could not survive spring conditions, and they do not start to grow at the wrong time of year. The temperature as well as the rainfall must be within certain limits for each species of annual plant to grow and bloom. Thus the summer annuals will not bloom in spring and the spring annuals will not bloom in summer.

How old is that saguaro?

Saguaros are famous for living a long time. But how long is that? Look at the different sizes of saguaros around you and notice how they change as they get larger. As you look at the stages of saguaro growth you can learn how to read their approximate ages. It's impossible to figure an exact age of any saguaro, but there are clues that tell you about how long a plant has been around.

As you learn about the life history of a saguaro, and look at the chart on pages 82 and 83, you will get an idea of the ages of the saguaros you see. To calculate how tall a saguaro is, stand next to one. You know your height. Let's say you are four feet tall and your name is Sandy. Have someone stand a short distance away and estimate how many "Sandys" high the saguaro is. A little math will give you a good idea of its height. Example: 6 Sandys high = 24 feet.

The development of the saguaro is extremely variable from one plant to another and from one location to another. The figures given here are averages only.

Babyhood

You probably will not see saguaros younger than about 10 years of age. They are growing under other plants and are too small to notice.

If your sharp eyes find a young saguaro about 6 inches (15.2 centimeters) tall it may be about 15 years old.

Look for a dense crown of stout spines shading the growing tip of the young plant. This reduces water loss and may protect it from being eaten. Short woolly hairs beneath the spines cover the top of the stem, further reducing moisture loss and protecting the plant against insects. The spines may help protect the plant from freezing.

Youngster

At about 30 or 40 years of age a saguaro is about 6 feet (1.8 meters) tall and additional ribs develop as the saguaro takes on a pickle shape. Look for new pleats that have been added to the stem. (For every pleat there is a woody rib inside.) Crowded spines surrounded by woolly hairs form a dense protective mat over the tip.

Young adult

The shape slowly changes and a bulge develops in the upper mid-section, giving the saguaro a bowling pin appearance. At about 50 years of age a saguaro is about 10 feet (3 meters) tall. The top spines change during this period of growth. They are now shorter and a mass of woolly hairs surrounding each spine is seen. This dense mat protects the top from freezing. This is where the first flowers will appear and the wooly spines may also protect the flower buds. When you see this fuzzy growth at the top, you know that the saguaro is at an age where it will grow flowers. This can by anywhere from 35 to 65 years of age.

Mature adult

At about 65 the saguaro is nearing 20 feet (6 meters) in height. At this stage arms may begin to grow. Most arms appear at the fattest place on the bowling pin shape. One or more short arms can grow the same year. At this age the plant has developed the largest number of ribs — about 20.

Middle age

At about 80 years of age the curved arms are about as large as the central stem. It will keep on growing, but very slowly now.

Old age

As a saguaro reaches 150 years it is still growing, but very slowly. It may add on only an inch or two a year. A very old saguaro may live to be 200 years old or more.

To get a feeling of size of these desert giants, stand next to a grand old saguaro. Look upward along the pleated surface, up the neat rows of spines, up towards its very top. How long has it been standing here? Perhaps 200 years? Two hundred years or more of

Cool Fact!

Saguaros do not produce annual growth rings, so it is through observation over many years and the study of old photographs of a known site that scientists are able to make educated guesses about the age of a saguaro.

One of the oldest, largest saguaros known grew in Saguaro National Park, in the Rincon Mountains. It is estimated that "Old Grandaddy," as it was affectionately known, was over 300 years old when it died in the 1990's. It had more than 50 arms.

searing summer heat, cold winter nights, long periods of parched air to be followed by drenching summer storms. For all those years it grew and thrived and provided food and shelter for so many creatures that share its desert home.

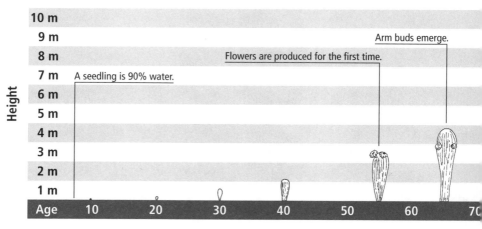

Height

10 m	
9 m	Arm buds emerge.
8 m	Flowers are produced for the first time.
7 m	A seedling is 90% water.
6 m	
5 m	
4 m	
3 m	
2 m	
1 m	
Age	10 20 30 40 50 60 70

Growth rates

The yearly growth rates of saguaros depend on many factors including age, location, temperature extremes, and the amount of rain.

Saguaros do not grow at an even pace throughout their lifetimes. Very young saguaros grow very slowly, perhaps only an inch (2.5 centimeters) per year. As they age the yearly growth rate increases. Saguaros in the 40 to 60 year age range are in their peak growing period and may add on 5 inches (13 centimeters) per year. Growth rates then begin to slow down. Saguaros in the 100 to 200 year age range may add only 2 or 3 inches (5 or 8 centimeters) per year.

The amount of rainfall is very important to saguaros' growth rates. The greater the average annual rainfall, the faster they grow. Saguaros growing next to washes or near streams may grow at a faster rate because of more water availability. Slope direction influences growth, too. The sun shines more directly on south facing slopes. North slopes receive less intense sunlight. Therefore saguaros growing on north, south, east, and west slopes will grow at different rates depending upon temperature. Saguaros growing at higher elevations may be subject to freezing which stunts growth.

So if you are looking for an easy formula to calculate a saguaro's age, you are out of luck. But children and adults alike are fascinated with saguaros and "How old is that saguaro?" is a common question. The graph below will help you make a rough age calculation. The heights represented are those of saguaros growing in Saguaro

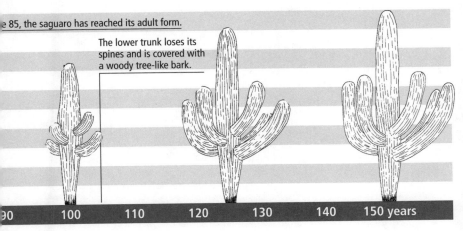

e 85, the saguaro has reached its adult form.

The lower trunk loses its spines and is covered with a woody tree-like bark.

90   100   110   120   130   140   150 years

Old Grandaddy

National Park's West District in the Tucson Mountains. This will give a semblance of average growth rates. Saguaros in Saguaro National Park's East Unit in the Rincon Mountains grow faster because of greater annual rainfall, and saguaros growing in Organ Pipe Cactus National Monument in the drier, hotter southwestern part of Arizona grow at a slower rate.

Where are the baby saguaros?

You may think there are no young saguaros around, but as you walk along look under the small bushes, trees, or within the crevices of rocks. Do you discover a small saguaro hidden in the shady cover of another plant?

Years ago a seed landed here. Maybe a fruit fell from a nearby saguaro and the seeds scattered. Perhaps a bird or a coyote ate saguaro fruit and the seeds were dropped in its scat. In this protected spot the tender seedling was shaded from the hot summer sun, blanketed from the cold on freezing winter nights, and hidden from a hungry packrats.

A little saguaro grows very slowly. Much of its growth is taking place in the roots. As the cactus grows it develops its protective waxy armor and eventually its spiny crown pushes up through the nurse plant that has shielded it for so many years. Look around and notice how many saguaros are poking out of other plants of the desert scrub.

A good place to find baby saguaros and other small cactuses such as pincushions and hedgehogs is under bursage plants. Bursage is one of the most common small shrubs carpeting our desert floor, but because it is not very showy, you may not notice it. Look for a small shrub with gray-green triangle-shaped leaves. Ball-shaped seeds with hook-like spines may be attached to the plant, and to your socks if you brush by it.

Cool Fact!

Any plant that shades a cactus or any small plant is called a "nurse plant." The larger plant is not really doing any nursing. It just happens to provide a good protected spot for a fallen seed to germinate. The little cactus did not seek out the protection. The seed happened to land in a spot that had the right conditions for growth. Most seeds never develop because they landed in places that were not protected.

Where can we find a saguaro boot?

You probably heard about saguaro boots laying around the desert. What are they and how can a saguaro have a boot? What is boot-shaped that might be a part of a saguaro. Here is a clue. Look at the saguaros that have woodpecker nest holes. If you see a dead saguaro you may see a boot-shaped woody structure among the woody ribs.

Saguaro boots, or pieces of them, may be seen in the remains of a large, fallen saguaro. Occasionally a boot can be seen in a standing saguaro skeleton, still attached to the ribs.

These are not really boots, of course, but because of their shape they have been given the name. What you see is the scar tissue, or callus, formed when a woodpecker made its nest cavity. Plants produce woody scabs over wounds, just as people produce scabs of dried blood over wounds. In both cases the scab forms a kind of protective bandage. Saguaros produce a tough, thick, woody scar tissue as the woodpecker digs into the cactus. These cavities are shaped somewhat like a shoe or boot. After a saguaro dies, the soft inner tissue soon dries and falls away from the woody skeleton onto the ground, eventually becoming part of the soil. The woody skeleton remains for many years until the termites finally eat the wood. The scab that formed around a woodpecker nest is so thick and hard that it lays on the desert ground for many years.

Often the boots are broken with the fall of a heavy saguaro, but if you see the skeleton of a saguaro lying on the ground, examine it. You may see a boot still attached to the wooden ribs, though chances are only pieces remain. Look and enjoy your discovery, but don't take the boot home because it is still an important part of the desert, providing shelter for the small creatures such as insects, spiders, and scorpions. And, remember, it is against the law to remove desert plants, dead or alive, from any public place, and only with permission from private land owners.

Some Indian groups used the boots from saguaros and another giant cactus, the cardón, to carry food and water.

Why are so many saguaros growing on one hillside, and hardly any on the opposite hillside?

As you look at the hills around you, you soon become aware that some hillsides have dense stands of saguaros, and other hillsides have very few. Why the difference? What do you notice about the saguaro-covered hillsides as compared to those with fewer saguaros? Try this on a sunny day. Look at two hillsides — one with many saguaros and the other with few. Hold out your hands so that the back of one hand is lined up with one hillside, and the back of the other hand is lined up with the other hillside. Look at the palms of your hand. Which one is being warmed by the sun? Now look at the hillsides. Which has more saguaros? The warm, sunny hill, or the cooler shadier hill?

As you feel the sun's heat on your hands and relate that to the hillsides you see before you, you discover that the hillside with the more direct sunlight has the thicker growth of saguaros. That tells us something about the needs of the saguaro. This cactus grows well in hotter conditions, and not as well in cooler situations. Think about winter when the sun stays low in the sky. Then the north-facing hillsides receive very little of the sun's warmth. On very cold nights temperatures drop below freezing, and the shady north slopes remain cold into the next day. Saguaros, especially young ones, do not do well in freezing weather, and die if temperatures remain freezing for many hours.

The direction a hillside faces causes that surface to be warmer or cooler, sunnier or shadier, drier or wetter than slopes facing other directions. It all depends upon the angle of sunlight. These different conditions create different habitats for plant life. As you travel, it is fun to notice the different plant growth on north, south, east and west facing slopes. This is true everywhere, not only in the desert.

Cool Fact!

89

Other plants are more suited for the shady, cooler slopes. You may notice more shrubs and low growing plants covering the ground on the north facing hills.

Why is that saguaro leaking brown stuff?

You see a saguaro that's not looking very healthy. A dark brown tar-like substance is oozing from holes in the skin and staining its side and dripping onto the plants and ground at the base of the cactus. If you can get close, examine where the "tar" is coming from. Are small insects flying around the area?

You will notice the brown ooze is coming from openings on the stem. The saguaro has suffered an injury. Perhaps the moist tissue was frozen during a very cold winter. Maybe there was some other kind of damage that was too extensive for the saguaro to cover with its woody callus. The dying tissue is now being eaten by insects that feed on dead plant material. That's what the oozy stuff is: rotting plant material being eaten by insects and other small organisms.

You will probably observe insects swarming around the rotting cactus flesh. They are coming in to eat the dead tissue, and have nothing to do with the cause or the spread of the ooze.

When any living thing dies, many insects and other organisms quickly move in to eat the dead material. It's a natural and important part of the recycling process.

Usually a plant that is leaking the smelly, brown ooze is dying. Occasionally one will heal and survive.

Cool Fact!

For many years it was thought that the decaying tissue was the result of disease caused by a bacteria, but now we know this is not the case. Physical damage must happen first — usually freezing. If there is a cold snap when the temperature falls below freezing for many hours, the moist tissue in the plant freezes and dies. But quite a few years pass between the frost and the appearance of the brown ooze. Therefore, we did not associate the dying cactus with the deadly freeze and assumed it was a disease.

Where do saguaros come from?

As you look at the saguaros along the trail, you wonder how they got there? They are so big. Did someone plant them? Most of the year you can't find clues to their beginnings. But during the months of May, June, and July you will notice interesting things happening at the tips of the main stems and arms of saguaros. In May and June look for big, white, waxy flowers. Later in June and into July look for the fruit, first green, later bright scarlet red. Hidden in the flowers and fruit are the answers to your question.

Saguaros are so immense and special to us that we sometimes forget that they carry on the same life processes as other plants. What is difficult to imagine is that those huge cactuses came from tiny seeds, about the size of a poppy seed.

Towards the end of April, flower buds resembling little green bumps appear on the tips of the stems and arms of larger saguaros. By mid-May the buds have grown large and are ready to open. The large, white, waxy flowers open at night a few hours after sunset. During the night, bats and moths come to the flowers to feed. They eat the powdery, yellow pollen or drink the sweet nectar. When morning comes, the bats and moths go away to sleep and birds and insects now feed from the flowers. As animals reach into the flowers to feed, some of the pollen sticks to their heads. As they fly from saguaro flower to saguaro flower some of this pollen falls onto the other flowers and pollination occurs. The bats, birds, and insects are pollinating the flowers, which means the transferred pollen will fertilize the flower and it will produce seeds.

During the day, the saguaro petals close. The hotter the day, the faster they close.

The showy flowers have done their job and will not open again. They have been pollinated and deep within the base of the flower, seed production begins. The old flower petals dry up and the base of the flower swells as the fruit develops. It is green at first, then about a month after flowering the fruit turns a bright scarlet red. The outer husk bursts revealing a mass of red pulp and small, black seeds. Woodpeckers, doves, Curve-billed Thrashers, House Finches and many other birds perch on the saguaros and eat the fruit. Some fruit falls to the ground. Coyotes, javelinas, rabbits, ants, squirrels, packrats, kangaroo rats, quail, and tortoises are some of the animals who join in the summer feast.

With all these animals eating the fruit and seeds, you might think that no seeds are left to grow. Not all seeds are eaten, and even those that are eaten may not be lost. The seeds pass through the digestive systems of some of the animals and are contained in their scat. Seeds that are eaten by kangaroo rats and a few other animals are too damaged to grow, but seeds that pass through other animals are undamaged. So the animals get nutrition from eating the fruit, then drop the seeds in little fertilizer packets throughout the desert. Some seeds will land in just the right spot and will germinate, or sprout, and a new saguaro begins its life.

Each saguaro fruit contains about 2000 seeds. An old saguaro will have yielded many fruits each year for many years. In the lifetime of an average saguaro it will have produced hundreds of thousands of seeds. A few seeds will land in places where rainfall, temperature, and protective cover are favorable and they will germinate. Perhaps one will survive to old age, replacing its parent.

Cool Fact!

Why is the top knocked off that saguaro?

It is common to see a saguaro with its top missing. Notice the height of those flat-topped saguaros. Is the flat top about the same height as a woodpecker hole would be found? Or perhaps the saguaro's lopped off top is much lower. What type of injury may have occurred that would weaken the stem of a saguaro and cause the top part to topple?

There are a number of reasons for a saguaro to lose its top. One is woodpecker nests. (Look at the question **Who made the holes in the saguaros?** to learn more about the woodpeckers that make the holes.)

Two species of woodpeckers are the hole drillers, but each carves out a different kind of hole. The smaller Gila woodpecker excavates a smaller hole that usually takes up a space between the outer skin and the ribs, and does not cut into the ribs. But the Gilded Flicker digs out a much larger nest hole higher on the saguaro where the woody ribs are thinner. It cuts right through the ribs and its nest may take up most of the inner part of the saguaro. Where there were once ribs and tissue now there is mostly open space. As you may guess, this weakens that part of a saguaro, and sometimes the top falls off, perhaps taking the woodpecker nest with it.

Another cause of toplessness may be freezing. Saguaros do well in the heat, but aren't able to survive many hours of freezing. Perhaps, years ago, there was a cold night where the temperature went way below freezing or remained below freezing for a day or so.

When the growing tip of a saguaro is injured, the saguaro may send out new arms near the damaged spot, even though it may not be the usual height to grow arms. This is a good strategy. The top of a saguaro produces flowers, fruit, and seeds. A damaged top can't do this, but arms can. So reproduction carries on.

The freeze may not have been severe enough to kill the whole plant, but it could damage the tender growing tip. Perhaps this left a weakened area that could not support the weight of the later growth.

There may be other factors as well. Sometimes there is injury near the top of a smaller saguaro: pack rat munching, or an unthinking person does something to damage the top.

Lightning does not knock the top from a saguaro — the heat broils the plant instantly and damage is so severe there is no chance of recovery.

Why do so many desert plants have spines?

Examine the branches and leaves of different plants. Cactuses have spines. Many trees and shrubs such as ocotillos, acacias, palo verdes and mesquites have woody thorns or sharply pointed twigs. But creosote bushes, jojobas, and many other desert plants do not have any sharp parts. How might spines be important to cactus? Notice how spines offer shade to the green skin. Look for signs of animal bites on prickly pears, chollas, even saguaros. Do you think spines would keep animals from eating a cactus? If you have been poked by a sharp thorn or had to remove a spiny cholla stem from your skin, you may think all desert plants are out to get you. You may guess that spines protect plants from hungry animals? But what about the many plants that do not have spines? What do the spines do for a plant?

Cactus spines may keep humans from getting too close, but many desert animals are not completely discouraged by spines. Packrats and javelinas chomp away at prickly pear and cholla cactus. Packrats climb right up onto the prickly pear cactus pads and nibble around the spines. They eat the fleshy cactus and the spines drop to the ground. Javelinas eat spines and all. Rabbits, coyotes, ground squirrels, tortoises, and insects eat cactus fruit which are covered with sharp, tiny stickers called glochids without any problems. Cactus Wrens and Curve-billed Thrashers use the spiniest chollas for their nests. Packrats carry spiny cholla stems to use in nest construction. Spines do deter, but do not prevent animals from eating the plants.

Cactus spines, which are actually modified leaves, seem to aid plants in a number of ways.

- **Spines shade the stem.** Look for little pincushion cactuses. They are commonly found growing under the branches of shrubs. The whitish-gray spines grow so thickly you can't even see the green cactus beneath.

- **Spines act as wind breaks** near the fleshy stems, which reduce water loss. The mat of spines on the tops of many cactuses insulate the tender growing tip against freezing and sunburn.

• **Spines play a role in reproduction.** The stems of chain fruit (jumping) cholla and teddy bear cholla easily detach. When a deer, coyote, javelina, or you brush against the cactus, the sharp, hooked spines attach to the passerby and the cactus stem is carried off. Finally it falls to the ground where it may root and grow.

Spines can be a problem for people, but if you become desertwise and follow a few common sense rules, you shouldn't get into a sticky situation.

1. Stay on the trail.
2. Don't swing your arms and accidently hit a spiny or thorny plant.
3. If you back up to take a picture, look where you are walking.
4. Remember that comb in your pack? If you do get a piece of cholla stuck on you, flick it off with a quick up and out motion.

Why is Kleenex stuck to that cactus?

Sometimes you notice what looks like old tissue or cotton stuck onto a prickly pear or cholla cactus. Carefully touch it and be careful not to get spines in your finger. How does it feel? Use a tiny twig to gently poke into the white mass. Can you find a small insect nestled within?

The white coating may look like wet tissue was blown onto the cactus stems, but it was made by a small scale insect, the cochineal.

The whitish, webby coating feels waxy. Beneath this protective waxy coat tiny insects are hidden. They can't be seen unless you carefully remove a bit of the covering. There you will find the red, wingless female cochineal insects. These are scale insects that have sucking mouth parts. They stick their beaks into the cactus and feed on the juices.

The female cochineal makes the webby, waxy coating. It protects her, the eggs, and young from the dry air and from predators. The tiny males, which are seldom seen, have wings but no mouthparts.

They are short-lived and their job is to mate with the females. A few cochineal are not harmful to the cactus.

Though we want children to respect animals and not do them harm, parents may wish to make an exception here for the sake of discovery. Trying this demonstration is up to your discretion. Because of the proximity of spines involved, this is best done by adults and older children. Using tweezers or a twig, carefully extract a cochineal insect from under the white covering and squish it between your fingers. You will be amazed to discover your fingers turn a brilliant scarlet. The red liquid contained within the insect may be a protection against predators.

Cochineal webbing is especially prominent on prickly pear cactus pads situated along busy streets. Perhaps the stress of city air weakens the cactus and the cochineal insect is better able to take up residence.

Cool Fact!

The cochineal insect has had quite an impact in history. Long before Europeans came to the New World, Native Americans of South and Central America, and the land that is now Mexico farmed and harvested the insects for red dye. They dried the female insects, extracted the red color, and made a crimson dye to color their clothing. When the Spaniards arrived they learned about the red dye and sent dried cochineal insects back to Spain. Soon the red coloring was used in cloth and paintings throughout Europe. Its use returned to America and it colored foods, beverages, and medicines. Today cochineal is still used in cosmetics, medicines, art supplies, and some foods. Read the label the next time you have a bottle of pink grapefruit juice. The pretty color may have come from cochineal.

What are those balls on the creosote bush?

As you examine the creosotebush you may notice marble-sized balls attached to the branches. In spring they may be green, other times of year they are brown. Take a close look. Examine with your hand lens. What are the balls made of? Do they look like masses of tiny leaves? What could cause a plant to form these interesting growths?

The round growth is a gall. The leafy ball attached to the stem was caused by a tiny fly. There are many different species of insects that make galls on creosote bushes; each species makes a slightly different kind of gall. The creosote woolly gall and the creosote midge gall are two common gall makers. There are perhaps a dozen species of flies which make galls on creosote bushes. Galls do not weaken the host plant. How does a tiny fly make these strange balls? The female fly lays eggs on a branch bud. The larvae hatch and feed on the plant. The plant responds to this by growing a gall of leafy material around the larvae. As the larvae grows, the gall grows larger. Within the ball of deformed creosote

Cool Fact!

Galls can be caused by many kinds of insects on many kinds of plants. Next time you are walking among oak trees look for galls on branches and leaves. Those galls are usually made by wasps.

bush leaves the larvae are protected against the hot, dry air, and from being eaten by animals, because many animals do not eat the resinous leaves.

Scientists aren't sure if the plant forms the gall because of the chewing of the larva or if some chemical was injected into the plant by the adult fly. Perhaps it's a combination of both.

100

What is the strange tan glob stuck on this branch?

Our eyes and brain zero in on things that seem different than their surroundings. This capsule-shaped "glob" attached to the branch does not look like it is part of the plant. This is a good time to use your magnifying lens. Do you see a row of tiny holes along middle of the capsule arranged so that they look somewhat like a zipper? Does the capsule seem light, as if it is made of hardened foam? Are tiny round holes dotted along the sides? What do you think produced this interesting structure?

This is the egg case of an insect called a praying mantid.

Some kinds of insects deposit their eggs within protected places such as plant tissue or in the ground; others deposit their eggs in unprotected places, such as on the surface of plants where they are exposed to weather and predators. Those insects have the ability to secrete a fluid that protects the eggs and glues them in place. The female praying mantid secretes a gummy liquid on a branch, twig, or stem. She beats the liquid to a froth with the tip of her abdomen. Before this foamy mass hardens she lays her eggs in a row of chambers, complete with escape hatches for the hatchlings to emerge. This usually happens in late summer or fall. The once frothy foam becomes a hard insulated egg case, called an oothecae.

Praying mantids are predatory insects that spend their time perched on leaves or along branches. There are different species of mantids and each kind is colored and shaped for a well-camouflaged match with its surroundings. It stands on its back four legs, holding up the large, powerful, toothed front legs in a praying position as it waits for an insect to walk by. Large eyes protruding from a very moveable head keep watch. When an insect comes near the praying mantid swiftly grabs it, holds it firmly with its strong front legs, and munches its meal.

Cool Fact!

The protective capsule remains firmly attached to the branch throughout the winter. In spring the eggs hatch within the capsule and miniature mantids emerge. These insects do not go through a larva and pupa stage, so the young look like tiny versions of their parents.

If the young emerge from the openings at the top, what made the tiny round holes along the sides? If you thought something was drilling in to eat the eggs, you are correct.

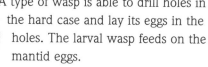

A type of wasp is able to drill holes in the hard case and lay its eggs in the holes. The larval wasp feeds on the mantid eggs.

What's happening to that dead tree?

You notice dead trees, cactuses, and shrubs here and there among the living plants. Why did the plants die? What may be some of the causes? Look closely at the wood of a dead plant. Do you see tiny holes? Pick at the bark. Do pieces easily come off? Do you notice grooves in the wood that appear to be made by insects? In late summer and fall look for dried mud covering dead twigs and grass, cactus skeletons, or on the woody base of a saguaro.

There are many reasons plants die: old age, uprooting by strong winds, lightning strikes, toppling from arroyo banks after the soil around their roots is washed away after a heavy rain. Maybe you can guess what caused a plant to die.

Soon after a plant has died, many kinds of insects are attracted to it. Tiny holes indicate where insects burrowed in. Larger holes may have been made by woodpeckers as they pecked to get at the insects.

Do you see dried mud covering the wood? Can you see hollow places within the wood where tunnels have been made? You might find hollowed out tubes of dried mud standing where termites have eaten away the dead grasses that had been inside the tubes. Termites are at work!

Termites are one of the few animals that eat cellulose — that's the strong, material in plants that give them structure. Trees, shrubs, grass, and cactus skeletons are mostly cellulose. Only fungi and tiny organisms called protozoans can chemically break it down. All termites contain protozoans in their guts. The termites chew up and swallow pieces of wood; within the termites' guts, the protozoans break down the swallowed material. The sugars contained in the cellulose can now be absorbed into the body of the termite with enough left over to feed the protozoans.

Cool Fact!

Termites are small, soft-bodied, whitish insects. Dead woody plant material is their food. There are many different types of termites. Some live in underground colonies and burrow through the soil in search of food. Others live within dead dry wood. The termite signs you are most likely to see are made by the encrusting termites. Examine pieces of dead wood, the woody bark at the bases of older saguaro cactuses, and dead grasses. Are they covered with a dried mud coating? The termites make this mud plaster coating and cement it all together with their saliva! The moist mud protects their soft bodies as they munch on the wood.

We do not want termites in our houses because they eat away at the wooden structure and can cause serious damage. But in the natural world they are important recyclers. By eating the wood, then eliminating their waste, the woody plant material returns to the soil. Because few other organisms can eat wood, there would be lots of dead plants piled up if it weren't for the termites.

Who made the holes in the saguaros?

Whether you are walking a trail through a forest of saguaro cacti or passing by saguaros growing in the middle of town you notice round holes in many of the plants.

What observations can you make? Where are the holes usually located? Are they all about the same size? Use your binoculars to get a closer look. Do you see any feathers stuck near the hole? Are the edges of the hole worn? Do you see a bird fly in or out of a hole? Do these clues help answer your question of who made the hole?

The holes were made by birds. Chipping into a tough, hard cactus requires a sturdy, sharp tool. The birds that have the right equipment for this job are the woodpeckers.

No, it's not Woody Woodpecker. He's the cartoon version of the Pileated Woodpecker which lives in cooler parts of our country. The two large woodpeckers that excavate the cavities within the saguaro are Gila Woodpeckers and Gilded Flickers.

The woodpeckers do not eat the cactus flesh. As they dig away at the cactus they flick the pieces of cactus from their beaks. If a woodpecker has recently been digging out a nest, you will see a black "eyebrow" over the hole. These are pieces of cactus that the bird flicked from its beak and got stuck above the hole. Living saguaro flesh is a whitish-yellow; it turns black when exposed to air.

Our bodies produce scabs over injuries which prevent us from bleeding to death, and plants produce a protective cover as well. The

Woodpeckers may reuse their old nest cavities, but many other species of birds may move into a ready-made house. Elf Owls, Screech Owls, and Pygmy Owls find these ideal homes as do many other birds such as Kestrels, Flycatchers, Purple Martins, House Finches, English Sparrows, and Starlings.

Gila Woodpecker

Gilded Flicker

saguaro produces a hard, thick, woody material over the damaged tissue. (See the entry Where can we find a saguaro boot?)

After the cactus flesh has dried and hardened inside the cavity, the female woodpecker lays three or more eggs on the bare floor of the nest. No nesting material is brought in.

Would this be a good place to raise young? Imagine you are a baby bird inside a saguaro nest cavity. When the outside temperature soars to over 100°F (38°C) you are nestled in a cooler 90°F (32°C) cavity, insulated by the saguaro's thick, moist tissue. At night when the outside temperature cools down, you stay warm because the heat that the saguaro absorbed during the day has now reached your nest. You are safe from predators, too. Notice that most nest holes are high up and only on tall saguaros. Within the safety of the nest the young birds feed and grow until they are able to fly away.

There's a pile of trash in that cactus!

Did some unthinking person toss a load of trash in the desert? Take a close look. What kinds of materials are in the pile? Is it in the midst of a prickly pear cactus or beneath a tree? Can you find trails leading into openings within the pile? This doesn't appear to be the work of humans, which means it must be the work of an animal. What do you suppose it is? Here's a clue. Has your mom or dad ever looked into your bedroom and announced it looked like a packrat lived there?

You are looking at a packrat house. The species that lives in the Sonoran Desert is the white-throated wood rat, but we will use the name packrat here. Although "rat" is in the name, this rodent is not related to the Old World rat we hear about living in dirty conditions in big cities. Packrats are very clean little animals.

Packrats aren't burrowers as are most other rodents. Instead they usually build their homes above ground, although they will also use openings in the sides of cliffs or arroyos. Packrats use all kinds of

construction materials: cholla stems, sticks, dried cactus fruit, pieces of trash people dropped, coyote and javelina scat and pieces of bone.

Do you see the packrat's trails leading into its den? If we could look inside we would find tunnels and chambers throughout the house. Food, which may consist of enormous numbers of seeds, is stored in some of the chambers. The sleeping area, the actual nest, is deep within the house at ground level. It is made of grasses or other soft material. The stickery packrat home may not look very comfortable, but the pile of old cactus, sticks, and other debris provide the packrat good shelter against the hot, dry desert climate.

Packrat dens can be huge, but these rodents live alone unless a female is caring for young. The young are sheltered and cared for within the nest until they are old enough to go out into the world to build their own homes. However, other animals also find packrat homes good places to live, including snakes, lizards, spiders, scorpions, and many insects.

Cool Fact!

Some packrats choose rock shelters for homes. In these protected places the plant and animal materials they bring in, as well as their food, remain dry. The urine of the packrats cement and preserve the plant material. When a packrat dies another will move in, add more material, and urinate on it. After thousands of years layers of preserved material have accumulated. As scientists examine these old middens, they find materials from junipers, oaks, and other cooler-climate plants, and bones from prehistoric animals — all clues to changes in the flora (plants), fauna (animals), and climate over thousands of years.

Qs and Clues:
Animals

Do you think we'll see any animals?

Read about the animals in your field guides and other reference books to help you learn favorable conditions for different species to be out and about. Some things to consider are:

What time of day is it: early morning, mid-day, evening?

What time of year is it?

What is the weather today: hot, cool, dry, wet?

Do some research about an animal you would like to see. Learn when it is active and likely to be seen. Is the animal diurnal (active during the day) or nocturnal (active at night), or crepuscular (active at dawn and dusk)? Will it be active in the hot or cool times of the day or year? Would it be more likely to be out after summer storms begin?

But if you do not see many animals, you will see signs that tell you the animals are here. What "signs" do animals make? Can you learn to read these signs?

Catching a glimpse of a coyote, deer, or javelina along the trail is exciting, but the small creatures are delightful finds, too. Take time to watch an insect crawling inside a flower, a spider in its web,

Cool Fact!

Many people mix up the words animal and mammal. Animals include all members of the animal kingdom. Invertebrates, such as worms, snails, insects, scorpions, and spiders, and vertebrates, the fish, amphibians, reptiles, birds, and mammals are all part of the animal kingdom. Any living thing that is not a plant, alga, fungus, or bacteria, is an animal. Some people say "animal" when they mean "mammal." Mammals are but one group of animals. Some mammal characteristics are: hair or fur, endothermic ("warm-blooded"), live birth, and the ability to nurse the young with milk. Coyotes, deer, javelinas, squirrels, and bobcats are a few of the mammals common in our desert. Oh, and don't forget humans — they are mammals too!

kit fox

or a bird singing from its perch. There is enjoyment and much to be learned from these observations, too.

If you don't see many animals, you will see signs that tell you that animals are nearby. Footprints, chew marks on plants, scat (droppings of waste material), holes in the ground, and nests are some animal signs to look for. Field guides are helpful tools as you play detective and put clues together to help you discover which animal was there and what it may have been doing. Look at the pages titled **"Which animal ate that cactus?"**, **"Eeeew animal poop!"**, and **"Snake holes!"** for hints.

Is that big bird an eagle?

Large birds soaring and circling above are common sights. Which birds are these? In order to figure this out carefully observe the a bird. Look for:
- silhouette (shape of body, wings, and tail against the sky)
- flight behavior (soaring, flapping)
- color and pattern of wings, body, and tail

The large birds you see flying over open desert areas are probably one of those described below. There are other large birds, so if none of the descriptions below match, look in your bird field guide. Also, immature birds look different than adults. Study the silhouette, flight, color, and patterns. These field marks will help you identify the bird.

Turkey Vulture

SILHOUETTE long wings; long feathers stick out finger-
   like from ends of the wings; small head
FLIGHT BEHAVIOR soars continuously; rarely
   flaps wings; may swoop low; wings usually
   held in broad V shape and a slight tilt
   upward (think V for vulture)
COLOR mostly black, flight feathers
   are silvery gray; head is red
SEASON They are seen from early March to mid-October in Arizona,
   then migrate south to Mexico in winter.
NOTE Vultures are NOT buzzards. Buzzards are Old World hawks
   that do not live in the Americas.

Red-tailed Hawk

SILHOUETTE broad wings, short tail; wings usually held
   straight out from body and not in a V shape
   as the vulture
FLIGHT BEHAVIOR soars, flaps occasionally
COLOR light breast; underwings light
   with black leading edges; top side
   of tail is bright red-brown which
   can be seen when the bird makes
   a turn

Red-tailed Hawk

Harris's Hawk

SILHOUETTE long legs, long tail

FLIGHT BEHAVIOR soars on flat wings and
glides on bowed wings (a slight downward curve)

COLOR head and body dark brown;
chestnut brown on front part of the
underwings; tail has a black band which separates the white tail
edge and white band near the body; note chestnut shoulder patch
and leg feathers on a perched bird

Raven
SILHOUETTE tip of tail is wedge-shaped; large bill
FLIGHT BEHAVIOR soars hawk-like, but also flaps;
  sometimes dives and "plays" with other
  ravens, and occasionally with vultures and
  hawks
COLOR solid black; sun may glisten on
  shiny feathers giving it a momentary
  bright or white look
VOICE often call with a loud "gronk" as they fly

Cool Fact!

Zone-tailed Hawks often soar with Turkey Vultures. At a distance they look just like the vultures, with similar color, size, and soaring behavior. But a look through binoculars reveals a feathered head and a white band on the tail. Ornithologists believe the mimicry is a way for zone-taileds to get food. Small birds are not wary of a flock of vultures overhead because they are not a threat, but they are alert for hawks soaring alone. A Zone-tailed Hawk can hide within a flock of vultures, check out the food supply below, then quickly fold its wings and plummet towards the ground where it may grab an unsuspecting dove.

Golden Eagle
SILHOUETTE very large; long, broad square-tipped
  wings
FLIGHT BEHAVIOR soars with wings in a
  very shallow, upward tilted V
COLOR all dark; golden mantle

What's that bird we hear?

You hear songs, chirps, tweets, and calls all along the trail. How can you tell which bird is making the sound? There are so many kinds of birds and some birds can make many kinds of sounds. When you hear a bird, listen carefully. Is it a song? Sing along with it. Maybe you can make up words to the song that will help you remember the tune and pattern of sounds. Is it a call? Again, make up words for what it seems to be saying. Or perhaps the sound reminds you of something. Use any trick you can to help you remember the call.

Wouldn't it be fun to be able to identify birds by their sounds? Use your listening skills to recognize the different songs and calls. On each walk learn a new call and the name of the bird making the call. With a little practice you will soon able to recognize our more common birds by their calls alone.

Here are some of the birds you are likely to see and hear along the trail as well as in your own back yard. Look at the COOL FACT to learn the difference between calls and songs.

House Finch
SONG musical up and down, conversational warbles with harsh
notes interspersed.
CALL a sweet *cheep*.

Mockingbird
SONG bubbling, sometimes gurgling or flute-like; repeats two or
three phrases and **pauses** between the phrases.
CALL a harsh *chock*.
NOTE This bird imitates other birds as well as noises of sirens,
squeaky doors, telephones rings,
etc.

Curve-billed Thrasher
SONG similar to the Mockingbird's but
with **no pauses** and little or
no repetition.

115

CALL a distinctive, very loud *whit-wheet?*, somewhat like a human whistle to attract attention.

Inca Dove
CALL a monotonous, repeated *coo-hoo* sounds somewhat like the bird is saying *no hope.*
NOTE When taking off on flight, the wings rustle like paper.

Mourning Dove
CALL a sad-sounding cooing, the last three notes are lower than the first... *COO-OOH, coo, coo-coo.* The mournful sound gives this bird its name.
NOTE The wings make a whistling sound when the bird takes off on flight.

White-winged Dove (a summer resident)
CALL a harsh, four syllable cooing... *ooooh OOO oooh OOO* which sounds as if the bird is asking, "Who cooks for you?"

Northern Cardinal
SONG a loud, melodious whistle with many variations including *cheer, cheer, cheer*, a rapid *woight-woight-woight-woight*, or *birdy-birdy-birdy.*
CALL a metallic *chip*

Pyrrhuloxia

SONG similar to the Cardinal, but thinner and shorter.

CALL a sharp *chink*

NOTE It is very difficult to differentiate between Cardinal and
Pyrrhuloxia calls.

Gila Woodpecker

CALL a loud, rolling *churrr*, a sharp *yip* and *kikikiki.*

Gambel's Quail

CALL a variety of sounds including cackling calls of one or two
notes, a wut wut, a sorrowful call that makes one think a bird got
its foot caught in a trap, and *chi-CA go go.*

Cactus Wren

SONG a low pitched *cha cha cha* or *chug chug chug*, sounding like
an old car trying to start on a cold morning.

Great-tailed Grackle

CALL a variety of shrill whistles, and loud clacks.

NOTE This bird is usually not found in desert growth, but is very
common in grassy city parks, ball fields, and golf courses.

When we hear bird songs, we think the birds are happy
because we often sing when we are happy. Ornithologists,
people who study birds, have not ruled out "happiness" or
"contentment" when birds sing, however, bird songs have
many functions. They may advertise:

"Here I am. I'll be a great mate!"

"This is my territory! Keep out!"

The call note, in contrast to song, is a brief sound with a simple structure.
It is usually one or two syllables with no more than four to five notes.
Calls may:

- be an alarm to warn of danger
- tell that food has been found
- tell location when a group has been separated
- keep a mated pair aware of each other's location
- be contact calls for young

The next three birds are common in our city parks. They are not native to North America. The Pigeon was brought to Nova Scotia by French settlers in the 1600s. English Sparrows and Starlings were introduced from England to the eastern U.S back in the 1800s. These birds have spread over North America, though they are generally confined to urban areas.

Rock Dove (the city pigeon)
CALL a deep, rolling, gurgling series of coo-roo-coos.
NOTE The wings clap when they take off in flight.

English or House Sparrow (actually a weaver finch)
SONG variations of *chiurp, chireep* and repeated scolding chatter.
CALL *chilup*

Starling
CALL a low-pitched, chirpy chatter without musical quality interspersed with whistles, clicks, squeals, squawks and a "wolf" whistle... *whooee*. It also mimics other birds.

If you want to learn more about identifying bird songs look in book stores and nature shops for tapes, CDs, and CD-Roms.

How can that bird stand on that cactus?

Birds are commonly seen perched on the top of saguaros or on very spiny cholla cactuses. Observe how birds are standing on all those **spines**. Are their toes grasping onto the spines? Are the toes in between the spines? Why aren't they getting poked?

Think about the legs and feet of birds. How are they different than yours? Unlike your fleshy feet, bird legs and toes are slender and covered with hard scales. Birds do not stand on the flat of the foot, but on their toes. That joint that looks like a knee bent backward is actually the heel. The knee joint is higher and hidden within the feathers. The thigh is also covered with feathers. Another advantage for cactus perching may be that the feet are made of tough tendons which have a limited supply of nerves and blood.

Cactus Wren

For all these reasons birds have no problem perching on spiny plants. They hold on to the spines with their long toes or just stand right on top of them without being hurt. Young birds, however, are not experts, and they must practice their standing-on-spiny-plants skills upon fledging (leaving the nest).

In addition, the thick feathery coats protect their bodies from the spines.

Desert birds and other desert animals have been living among spiny plants for countless generations and they have evolved into spine-wise animals, well adapted for living safely in a prickly habitat.

Which bird made that nest?

Study the nest and look for these clues:
- location of the nest (in which plant or structure)
- materials used to build the nest
- the size of the nest
- the shape of the nest
- other interesting features

Many species of birds live in the Sonoran Desert and many bird nests are difficult to see because they are hidden within tree branches and are well camouflaged. Different species of birds build different styles of nests. The three most common nests you are likely to see, no matter the time of year, are these:

Cactus Wren

LOCATION in cholla cactus, shrub, palo verde tree, or in the crotch of saguaro arms

MATERIALS straw colored grasses, sometimes bits of string and other trash

SIZE football-size, about 12 inches long

SHAPE football shape (with a hollow inside)

OTHER nest is usually tilted; the opening is at the upper end

Bird nests protect the eggs and young birds in many ways. The location and materials hide the nests from predators, the nest provides protection from heat, cold, wind, and rain. This is the birds' nursery: a place to be fed, to learn, and to develop instincts necessary for survival. The cactus wrens use nests throughout the year for roosting (sleeping) shelters.

Curve-billed Thrasher

LOCATION in cholla cactus or spiny shrub

MATERIALS thorny twigs, loosely woven

SIZE up to a foot in diameter

SHAPE bowl shape

OTHER look directly above the nest and notice the spines have been broken off by the adult birds

Verdin

LOCATION within thorny twigs at the end of a branch, also in crotch of cholla or tree branches; commonly found along arroyos

MATERIALS thorny twigs, densely woven

SIZE softball-size, up to eight inches diameter (large for a tiny bird)

SHAPE oval ball (with a hollow inside)

OTHER opening is near the bottom; about 2000 twigs may be used in one nest

During the spring nesting season never get close to a nest. If you use a mirror to point out the nest to someone, reflect the light on a nearby branch, not on the nest so that you do not disturb nesting birds. Other times of year you may get close for a better look at the nest, but leave the nest in place. Some birds reuse nests or recycle the materials. It is against the law to remove nests of many species of birds.

Now that you know how to identify the nests of three bird species, you can learn about other kinds of nests by using the observation clues and then doing research in a bird book, including the Desert Museum's *A Guide to Southern Arizona Bird Nests & Eggs*.

Look at all the tadpoles in the puddle! Where did they come from?

What a surprise to find tadpoles! We do not think about water creatures, such as amphibians in the desert, but there they are, swimming about in a little pool of water. How did they get there? What stages of development do you see — no legs, hind legs, all four legs? Are any tiny toad-like animals sitting along the edge of the pond? What will happen to them when the pond dries up?

It is during the summer rainy season when tadpoles appear in the ponds — literally overnight. Where do they come from? It may seem like magic, but it's not. The real story is more fascinating than magic.

The tadpoles you discovered may be spadefoot tadpoles. The adult amphibians have been living underground for most of the year. They burrowed under last fall at the end of the rainy season. There they remained, a foot or more below the soil surface. Their body functions slow way down. They need so little air that they can survive on the oxygen in the soil. They do not breathe with their lungs; instead, oxygen enters their bodies through the skin.

They spend fall, winter, and spring months underground. As summer temperatures heat the ground the spadefoots begin to move towards the surface. The summer storms arrive and the thunder along with the banging of the heavy raindrops on the surface of the ground signal the spadefoots to dig up and out of their burrows. The loud, sheep-like bleats you may hear on a wet summer night are the males calling the females. In countless rainpools spadefoot mating is taking place. The male grasps the female around the waist and fertilizes the eggs she lays. The next afternoon little tadpoles hatch!

Different spadefoot tadpoles have different diets. Some are herbivores and graze on algae and other plant material. Some are carnivores — actually cannibals because they feed on other tadpoles. What are the advantages and disadvantages of these two diets?

Because there is more energy in a meat diet, the carnivores grow quickly and have the advantage of developing before the pond dries up, but their quick growth leaves them with little fat stored in their bodies, thus a lower survival rate after leaving the pond. Herbivores have the disadvantage of a low survival rate in a fast drying pool, but those that swim in a long-lived pond are able to store a great deal of fat during a longer period of growth, thus they will be better able to survive outside the pond. Scientists are studying the differences between the herbivorous grazers and the carnivorous predators and why tadpoles take on different dietary lifestyles.

Spadefoot tadpoles eat a variety of plant and animal materials floating and swimming in their ponds, and they quickly grow — first the hind legs develop, then the front legs. Inner organs are changing, too. Air-breathing lungs replace gills. The digestive system also changes because the spadefoot's diet will change from the tadpole diet of pond organisms to an adult diet of insects.

It takes only a few weeks for a spadefoot to go from egg to air-breathing young adult, but it takes the leopard frog and bullfrog a year or two to make the change from tadpole to adult. However, these frogs live in places where there is permanent water, so the speedy metamorphosis from water-breather to air-breather did not evolve in those amphibians.

The rains stop in late summer. The hard spade-shaped projections on the spadefoots' hind legs help excavate as they dig themselves underground, back end first. There they remain until the summer rains come again.

Do you notice the words "toad" or "frog" were not used in the text? That is because spadefoots are not true toads. They are in a separate family. We have true toads in our desert, too. The common ones are red-spotted toads and the huge Sonoran Desert toad. There are leopard frogs near desert areas, too, but they need a permanent stream or pond for their survival.

What if a Gila monster chases us?

How big is a Gila monster? How big are you? Do you think an animal the size of a Gila monster would chase us? Or would the Gila monster be the one to run away? Do you think you might see a Gila monster? Where are they likely to be found along your walk?

You would be lucky, indeed, to see a Gila monster because most of their lives are spent within burrows or rock crevices. When above ground they quickly retreat into a hiding place at the first sense of danger. Gila monsters remain underground during winter and the hot, dry, early summer months. Most activity occurs in April and May and during the summer rains when they feed and breed, but even then, their time above ground may be less than an hour. In an entire year Gila monsters are above ground only one per cent of the time. These lizards are mainly diurnal (active during the day), but can be seen after dark during summer rains.

Gila monsters can dig their own dens, but often enlarge natural crevices or burrows made by other animals. Boulders and rocky terrain, desert trees and shrubs, and washes or arroyos are good habitat.

The Gila monster is venomous. In fact, it is the largest and only venomous lizard in the U.S. There is only one other venomous lizard in the world, which is the Mexican beaded lizard. These lizards do not inject venom through hollow fangs. The venom is contained in sacs in the lower jaw. As the Gila bites down, the venom is carried along grooves in the teeth and enters the wound as part of the saliva. The venom is usually not delivered in large enough quantities to be life-threatening to humans, though there are some deaths recorded. Most bites occur when people try to handle them. The strong jaws deliver a strong, tenacious bite.

The scent of prey is picked up by flicking the tongue which carries the smell to the roof of the mouth where it is transmitted to the Jacobson's organ (rattlesnakes do this, too). Very young cottontail rabbits, rodents, quail eggs, nestling birds, tortoises and other reptile eggs are all part of a Gila monster's diet. The strong jaws help in capturing, grasping, and consuming prey. Large quantities of food can be consumed at one time — over a third of the body weight, but few meals are needed because of their slow metabolism (bodily processes) and long periods of inactivity. Excess fat is stored in the tail and used to supply energy during inactive times. Most of the water comes from food, but they will drink when water is available.

Although this lizard is usually slow moving, it can lunge at a predator or quickly spin around to face an attacker. Little is known about predators, but they are possibly mountain lions, coyotes, and large hawks. Gila monsters have lived in captivity over 30 years, but the life span in the wild is unknown.

Gila monsters are feared by people who do not understand them. What is it about these lizards that creates fear? Perhaps it is the large size — they may be as long as two feet (60.8 centimeters) from nose to tail tip — and their venomous bite. The hard, bright pink and black beaded skin is unusually gaudy. Another possible reason for fear is in the name — *monster*. (Its cousin to the south, the Mexican beaded lizard, is better named and not so feared.) These may be some of the characteristics that have prompted people to invent wild stories about the Gila monster, making it seem as if this lizard is some kind of alien creature with special powers.

The misunderstood Gila monster is the subject of more superstitions, myths and legends than most other desert creatures. Except for its large size and venom glands, the Gila monster is similar to other lizards. The best way to conquer a fear of something is to learn more about it. There are many untrue stories about Gila monsters.

Here are the FACTS behind some common myths:

- Gila monsters DO NOT spit poison,
- DO NOT breathe out poisonous vapors,
- DO NOT need to roll on their backs to bite,
- DO NOT wait until sundown or thunder to let go if they do bite someone, and
- the forked tongue IS NOT a stinger.

- They DO eliminate body wastes.

The real information about desert animals is more interesting than the myths, but scary stories persist. Some people believe them, thus they unnecessarily fear and loathe this misunderstood lizard.

Gila monsters and Mexican beaded lizards are the only reptiles with armored hides and forked tongues. The "beaded" scales are rounded, each covering a bump of bone. The scales on the underside of the head, body, and tail are flat.

Because the Gila monster fascinates and frightens people, many are captured by collectors or killed by people who misunderstand them. Therefore the Gila monster is protected by Arizona state law —it is against the law to harm them or keep them without a permit.

Now that you know about these interesting lizards, they don't seem so scary, do they? Remember their habitat requirements and times of activity and keep a sharp eye open. Maybe you will see one on your walk in the desert.

Look, a lizard!

Your sharp eyes spot a lizard. What caused you to see it? Perhaps it moved and that is what caught your attention. Is it easy to see when it is standing still? Or does its cryptic coloration camouflage the lizard? Is it in the sun or shade? Is it still or bobbing up and down? Is it eating or appear to be looking for food? These observations will help you learn some things about lizards.

Lizards are among the most commonly seen animals in our desert, but it is always fun to spot one darting across the trail or perched on a rock. Most lizards have remarkable cryptic coloration. This means they are camouflaged. Chances are the lizard's movement attracted your attention. When they are still, they are almost impossible to see. Notice how the color and pattern make it almost invisible against its background. In fact, when you try to point out the lizard to someone else, that person may have a difficult time finding it. Use your little mirror and aim the reflected light near, but not on, the lizard to point it out to others.

greater earless lizard

Clark spiny lizard

Many lizards are diurnal — they are active during daytime. Reptiles, amphibians, fish, and invertebrates do not have an internal temperature control as do birds and mammals. They rely on their surroundings for heating and cooling. They do this in a number of ways. During cool times they absorb heat by basking in the sun. During hot times they stay in the cooler shade. While foraging for food they move from shade to sunlight to shade, keeping their body temperatures within a comfortable zone. Over hot

zebra-tailed lizard

ground they stand tall so they are not overheated. When they need warmth they lie on a warm surface.

In colder months you will not see lizards. They are in a dormant state, at rest in burrows. The cool temperatures have caused their body processes to slow way down. Underground they are protected from predators and freezing air temperatures.

The horned lizard's gray and tan colors and blotchy patterns serve as excellent cryptic cover, but the fringy scales around the edges of the flat bodied lizards help conceal them as well. Because of those edge scales there is no definite line between the lizard and its background. Not only are horned lizards hard to see, but many predators would not have an easy time eating such thorny creatures.

Is the lizard bobbing its head or doing pushups on top of a rock? These are some of the ways lizards communicate with one another — with body language rather than sounds. Perhaps it is telling another lizard "This is my territory!" or "I'm the head lizard around here."

There are many species of lizards you will see. If you want to learn to identify them, pick up one of the reptile field guides listed in the Bibliography. Here are a few common lizards to look for:

Zebra-tailed lizards will catch your attention when they wag their black and white banded tails. A predator looking for lizard lunch may be distracted or confused by the display, or if it does pounce, it may grab the very visible tail. As is true with many lizards, the tail breaks off and the rest of the lizard runs to safety.

lesser earless lizard

Whiptail lizards can be noisy as they hunt for prey. If you hear rustling noises under leaves and other ground cover look for a long-tailed, slender, dark-colored lizard thrashing among the undergrowth in search of insects.

"Horny toads" are really lizards, but their flattened bodies look somewhat toad-like. The diets of many species of **horned lizards** consist of ants, and they can sometimes be seen alongside anthills, lapping up ants with their sticky tongues.

Interestingly, most people like lizards yet fear their reptilian cousins, the snakes. Our fascination with lizards is evident in the lizard designs on jewelry, pottery, t-shirts, and other artwork, as well as on prehistoric artifacts.

collared lizard

Are those snake holes?

You notice many round holes in the ground. Your first thought may be "snake holes," but are they? Examine them.

Notice the sizes of the holes. Where are they located? Do you find them under bushes and trees? Do you see them in mounds of dirt? Can you see spider webs in them? Are there trails or tracks leading to and from the hole?

Look for holes along cliffsides, especially in arroyos. Now study the ground. Is it rocky and hard? Or is it sandy and soft? Think of a snake's body. Would a snake be able to dig into the soil?

Many of the holes you see were excavated in very hard, dry, rocky soil. Could a snake do this? You need a shovel to dig in this hard ground. Animals need digging tools, too. Their tools are feet and toenails. Snakes lack these digging tools, therefore they aren't capable of digging holes. But, could a snake be in one of these holes? Yes, it could. Snakes, spiders, centipedes, scorpions, insects, and lizards are but a few animals that would find a shady burrow a good place to hide away from hot days, cold nights, and predators.

So who's making all these holes? Here are some of the animals who dig burrows along with descriptions of their burrows. Do the burrows you see match any of these?

Kangaroo rat

Many holes in a mound of soil, often in the shade beneath a plant, tell us this is probably a kangaroo rat burrow. The holes are oval shaped, about 3 inches (7.5 cm) in diameter. Look for trails leading to the burrow. It may seem as if many kangaroo rats live here, but unless a female is raising young, there is only one kangaroo rat living in a burrow.

131

Pocket mouse

You may discover another group of holes under a shrub or near rock. These won't be in a mound of dirt, but on the flat ground. If the holes are 1–1.5 inches (2.5–3.8 cm) across and perhaps show tracks indicating a little animal was scurrying in and out, you are probably looking at the home of a pocket mouse, a close relative of the kangaroo rat.

Packrat

Along an arroyo you may see many burrows of all sizes dug into the cliffside. Carefully look into the burrows. Use your mirror and shine reflected sunlight into the dark burrow. Do you see piles of sticks, cactus pieces, rocks, and other debris? Do you see small black scat (animal droppings)? This is the home of the packrat (white-throated woodrat). However these burrows are also used by rock squirrels, tortoises, snakes, spiders, and countless insects and other small creatures. The packrat makes another kind of home, too. Read about it under the entry, **There's a pile of trash in that cactus!**

Harris antelope ground squirrel

Holes 2–2.5 inches (5–6.3 cm) across in rocky soil in saguaro/palo verde habitats could be the home of the bushy-tailed, side-striped Harris antelope ground squirrel.

Round-tailed ground squirrel

The round-tailed ground squirrel, a tan, unmarked squirrel with a thin, round tail makes burrows in flat, open, sandy desert areas

The funnel-shaped holes you find in sandy or soft soil are made by insects — antlion larvae. The immature insects make the holes and hide just under the soil at the bottom of the funnels. Ants or other crawling insects that come too close to a trap fall into the funnel and tumble to the bottom. This triggers the jaw of the antlion larva waiting below. It grabs the prey with strong jaws and devours the prey. You will probably not see the larvae because they are beneath the soil surface, but you have probably seen the winged antlion adults. These lacy-winged insects are common around porch lights on summer nights.

(and city parks). The holes are 2 to 2.5 inches (5–6.3 cm) in diameter; there may be many holes in mounds of dirt. These squirrels are often mistaken for prairie dogs.

Spiders

It's hard to believe that spiders can excavate burrows into the hard packed desert soil, but their strong, long fangs make good digging tools. Most spiders live above ground — you are familiar with their interesting webs. But some species spend most of their lives in their underground shelters.

Tarantula

Look for an almost perfect circle 1–1.5 inches (2.5–3.8 cm) across, often on flat ground and out in the open. This is the home of a tarantula. You will see some webbing over the entrance and if you walk up quietly you may see the hairy legs of the tarantula near the opening. It will make a quick retreat into the burrow when it detects your presence. You will find tarantula burrows from April to October. In winter the holes are completely covered with webbing. Dirt, leaves, and other debris stick to the webbing and the holes are impossible to see.

Wolf spider

Wolf spiders are burrowers, too. The opening is different from that of the tarantula. It is less than 1 inch (2.5 cm) across and a collar of leaves, twigs, and other and debris surrounds the hole.

Trapdoor spider

The door of the trapdoor spider is extremely difficult to see; it looks exactly like the surrounding soil. This burrowing spider constructs a door of desert soil, silk, and saliva which covers the burrow. The door is hinged to the burrow wall with webbing. The spider spends most of its life just under the door, waiting for a meal. When an insect walks by, the trapdoor spider scoots out, pounces on its prey and drags it inside, closing the door behind it.

Antlion

Another type of "hole" is found in sandy or very fine soil. Look for funnel-shaped holes about 1–2 inches (2.5–5 cm) across the top and 1−2 inches (2.5−5 cm) deep. These depressions are the traps of the antlion larvae. See the Cool Fact for more about the antlion.

Besides holes, other clues of animal life can be found on the desert floor. Here are more animal signs to look for.

Cottontails and jackrabbits

Desert cottontails do not do much burrowing except when they have young. Jackrabbits do not burrow at all. But these animals do leave their marks. Cottontails will scrape away the soil in a shady spot under a cactus, shrub, or tree or wash bank and rest there during the warm part of the day. Jackrabbit scrapes will be under creosote bushes and low shrubs in open flat areas. Branches clipped at rabbit height many be another sign.

Dust baths

Perhaps you spot round dusty places where the rocky ground cover is disturbed and the softer soil beneath the rocks are exposed. These are bird baths! Many birds, especially quail, scratch out areas in the pebbly ground cover, exposing dusty soil beneath. They clean their feathers by wriggling in these depressions and tossing dust over their backs. The dust absorbs the extra oil and may also rid them of parasites living in the feathers.

Snake rest

Occasionally you will find a very round, shallow depression in the soil with a rim of soil and pebbles along the edge. In softer soil you

may actually see marks that look like the coils of a snake. And that is exactly what has happened. Rattlesnakes, especially, will coil and nestle into the soil. As they wriggle in, they push up some of the loose soil and pebbles around their bodies. They return to the same depressions repeatedly.

Soon you will be able to "read the dirt" and discover other animal signs.

134

What do we do if we see a rattlesnake?

You may walk many, many miles before you see a rattle-snake, and it is possible that you may never see one in the wild. Shadows, ground cover, and the snake's colors and pattern blend together so well that you could walk right by a snake and never see it. If you do see a snake, whether it is a rattlesnake or another kind of snake, stand back and observe. If the snake is lying quietly, notice its camouflage. If it moves, watch how it crawls along the ground. Where does it go? Memorize the pattern, then look in a reptile book to identify it.

As you walk along the trails, keep alert for a glimpse of a snake. Look under bushes, alongside boulders, or within rock crevices and you may spot a rattlesnake resting or waiting for prey to come by. Maybe you hear the rattle before you see the snake. Rattlesnakes DO NOT always rattle when they see humans, and a rattle DOES NOT mean they are about to strike. A snake's rattle can be quite loud, though the rattle of a smaller snake might resemble an insect's buzz.

The best thing to do if you see a rattlesnake is to enjoy the experience. Stand still and observe, but don't get too close. Stay back a few yards (meters). Get a good look at the colors and pattern. Notice the tail pattern. That may be a help in identifying the kind of rattlesnake, or at least narrowing it down to a few possibilities.

If the rattler moves, watch how it crawls along the ground. Do not fear that it will chase you; you are much bigger than the snake and it wants to get far away from you. Keep your eyes on the snake, because if you take your eyes away for a moment it will be hard to find again, the camouflage is so perfect. Does it crawl under the dense growth of a bush? Does it disappear into a hole in the ground?

The more commonly seen rattlesnakes of the Sonoran Desert are the western diamondback, Mohave rattlesnake, tiger rattlesnake, blacktail rattlesnake, and the sidewinder. A snake often mistaken for a rattlesnake is the gopher snake. It has a blotchy pattern made up of shades of brown and yellow, but it has a slender head and, of course, no rattle. However, gopher snakes can be good rattlesnake mimics. When they are on the defensive, they flatten their heads, hiss, and vibrate their tails so rapidly you actually hear a rattle-like sound.

Cool Fact!

You CANNOT tell the age of a rattlesnake by counting the number of rattle segments. Between sheddings a new segment develops beneath the skin next to the base of the rattle. Each time the snake sheds its skin the new segment is exposed. Snakes can shed a few times a year. As the snake moves about, segments wear and break off, therefore most wild rattlers have no more than ten segments. (Rattlesnakes in captivity don't move much and often have more.) If you observe a snake move, notice that the rattle is usually held vertically which may offer it some protection and keep it from inadvertently making sounds.

You noticed how well the color and markings camouflaged the snake. That emphasizes one of the reasons you must stay on the trails at all times. Snakes seldom waste their precious venom on things that are not food, but if you wander off the trail and step next to a resting rattlesnake, the snake could bite in self defense. That is an experience you do not want to have.

Snakes are a very important part of our environment. They eat such things as packrats, mice, rabbits, birds, lizards; some even eat other snakes, thereby keeping populations of those animals in check. There would be too many animals for the environment to support if it were not for snakes and other native predators.

Many people think of rattlesnakes when they think of deserts. Movies and television would have us believe that deadly snakes hide under every rock waiting to strike anyone who walks by. But now you know that is not true at all.

Look, a tortoise! Can we tell how old it is if we count the rings on the shell? May I pick it up?

A desert tortoise is one of the few animals you can observe at close range. You can stoop down and take a close look, but DO NOT PICK IT UP. Do you see the rings around each of the large scales that cover the shell? What do you think they tell us? Look at the part of the lower shell that sticks out under the tortoise's head. Is it long and turned upward, or is it small and not turned up?

Desert tortoises are not uncommon but seldom seen because they spend most of their lives in burrows. Even when they are out and about you could walk by a tortoise and not see it because it blends into the desert landscape so well and there is little movement to attract our attention.

It is tempting to pick one up because we know they won't hurt us. Resist that temptation. A tortoise stores water in its bladder. This water is not excreted as waste, but stays inside the tortoise and is reabsorbed back into the system to be used as needed. When a tortoise is picked up it senses danger and as a defense it releases the

water onto the molester. When this happens the tortoise has lost its reservoir of precious water. It may not rain for a long time, and giving up its water reserve could be a serious problem for the tortoise.

You may have heard the story about counting the rings on the shell scales to age a tortoise. That is one of those untrue tales. Notice the large scales that cover the top shell, or the carapace. Beneath these scales, or scutes, is the bony skeleton. As the tortoise grows, ridges are added to each scute. The rate of growth depends upon how much the tortoise finds to eat. In a dry year, when not much food is available, perhaps no growth rings develop. In a good year with lots of greens, a ring may be added. Old tortoises have spent many years crawling about under brush and into burrows and the rings on their scutes may be so worn they are difficult to see.

Tortoises seem to have a good sense of direction. They recognize landmarks, they can walk a straight line to their burrows, they know the locations of water and food sources, and they know where other nearby tortoises are.

If the tortoise is at least six inches in length, you may be able to tell whether it is male or female. Look at the part of the lower shell that sticks out under the tortoise's head. This is called a gular horn. If it extends out under the head and is turned upward, the tortoise is a male. Males often fight one another and use the horn to flip another male onto its back. If the horn is short and not turned up, it is a female. If you can get low to the ground and get a good side view, here is another indication of sex: the back part of the male's bottom shell, the plastron, is concave or curved inward. The female's plastron is flat.

138

Is that big black bee going to sting us?

A very large, shiny-black bee may buzz by. It may even circle around you a few times. Stand quietly and observe it. Perhaps you will see it land on a flower. Watch it as it crawls about the flower.

This is a carpenter bee. If one of these commonly seen bees buzzes by, you *will* see and hear it. These are our largest bees ...over an inch long. They look scary, especially when they fly around you checking you out. But they are not known to sting people unless someone swats or handles them. The male does not have a stinger.

As the bee crawls into flowers, pollen grains stick onto its very hairy body. As it flies from flower to flower, some of the pollen carried on the bee falls onto the pistils, thus pollinating the flowers, enabling them to produce seeds.

Carpenter bees have an interesting life cycle. The female chooses a nest site — a stalk of sotol, yucca, or agave, a piece of wood, or perhaps the wooden eaves of a house. Using her very strong mandibles (chewing mouth parts) she digs out a tunnel. She coats the tunnel with a paste of pollen and nectar. At the far end of the tunnel she lays an egg, then walls it off with a mixture of wood particles and saliva. She lays another egg and walls it off. She may lay over ten eggs, each protected within its woody chamber. Her job is done and she emerges from the tunnel entrance and flies away. When the eggs hatch, the larvae eat

the food paste. They grow and develop into pupae. The first eggs to be laid were fertilized and will be females. The last eggs to be laid were unfertilized and will be males. The males develop before the females even though they were laid last. As each adult bee emerges from its pupal state it chews its way out of its cell. The bee nearest the tunnel opening exits first, the second bee exits next, and so it goes until all the bees have emerged.

Cool Fact!

Observe carpenter bee activity around flowers. Often they do not crawl into the flower. Instead they chew a hole into the base of the flower and extract the nectar that way. In doing this they get the nectar, but they do not play a role in pollinating the flower. Hummingbirds and insects cannot get nectar from a flower that has been pierced by a carpenter bee.

Are there killer bees out here?

You are sure to see many kinds of bees and other buzzing insects on the trail as well is in your own yard. You hear about "killer bees" attacking dogs and people. How concerned should you be? What should you do if you see a bee visiting a flower? What should you do if you see a swarm of bees? All good questions. Some knowledge about the subject will help calm unnecessary fears and give you valuable advice on what to do in the event you do encounter a swarm of bees.

Do not be fearful of encountering Africanized bees (a better name for "killer bees") during your desert walks, but there are precautions to take and facts you should know about if you would find yourself in a potentially dangerous situation.

Watch and listen for bees along the trail. Some of the places bees may nest are in burrows and crevices along an arroyo, in a woodpecker hole in a saguaro, in a fallen tree, or in other hidden places. Chances are you will not encounter any swarms, but if it should happen this is what to do:

- If bees start flying around you, run as fast as you can in a straight line. Do not try evasive maneuvers like zigzagging. Do not stop running until the bees stop chasing you or you get to a safe place like a house. They will chase you for 100 to 150 yards, but you can outrun them.
- As you run use your shirt to cover your nose, mouth, and eyes.
- Do not swat at them. This will only make them more likely to sting.
- If you are stung do not pull out the stinger. This will only inject more venom. Instead, remove the stinger by scraping a knife, fingernail, or credit card, across the stinger.
- Africanized bees are attracted to dark colors and hair, so wearing light colored clothing is a good idea (it also keeps you cooler on a sunny day).
- Do not wear perfume or perfumed lotions. Perfume attracts many insects.

You cannot tell the difference between the European and African honeybees just by looking at them. It takes careful examination in a laboratory to determine the type of bee. Actually, entomologists (scientists who study insects) now consider all bees in the Southwest to be Africanized because the two kinds of bees have interbred. The venom of Africanized bees is no more potent than European bees; their danger lies in their aggressiveness. They are more likely to chase and attack someone who disturbs their nests and they attack in greater numbers.

Cool Fact!

Honeybees are not native to the Western Hemisphere. Early settlers brought honeybees to North America from Europe for honey and wax production. In 1956, honeybees from Africa were imported into Brazil because the African bees were better suited to the hot humid climate. They thrived and spread across South America, mating with and displacing the docile European honeybees, resulting in a hybridized bee we call the "Africanized" bee. The Africanized bees spread northward and in 1990 the first colony was found in the United States in Texas. By the mid-1990's they were in Arizona, and they continue to spread into the United States.

Many of the bees in urban areas are non-native honeybees. Native bees, especially ground-nesting bees, are displaced by city development. Also, since honeybee colonies are large (up to 40,000 individuals), they usually outnumber natives in urban areas.

If you are out hiking and see bees you can assess the risk by asking these questions:

- Are the bees feeding at flowers? If so, they are not likely to become aggressive, though an individual may sting if it is harassed.
- Are the bees coming out of a rock crevice or a tree hole? If so, they are at a nest. Hikers should stay well away because Africanized bees are very aggressive in defense of their nest. Because these animals become aggressive so easily, nests close to houses, stables, or kennels should be professionally removed.
- Are the bees clustered in a ball in a tree? If so, this is a swarm of bees which have stopped to rest while scouts look for a place to make a nest. Swarms usually are not aggressive, and leave in a day or two.

Insects, birds, and other animals that visit flowers for their nectar are very important. See the question, **Why are there bugs in the flower?** to learn more about this.

What's that big wasp with the orange wings?

A huge wasp with bright orange wings is a common sight in our desert. Even though it is the largest wasp you will see, it won't bother you. Observe it. Is it crawling around the flowers in a bush or shrub? Is it walking along the ground? Here's a hint. This wasp is known for its relationship with the tarantula.

This is the pepsis wasp, also known as the "tarantula hawk." If this wasp flies by, you will see it! It is BIG...almost two inches long. Not only is its size impressive, but the colors catch your eye, too. The body is a metallic blue-black and the wings are a very bright orange. Some species have blue-black wings.

In spring, when the palo verdes, mesquites, acacias, and milkweeds are in bloom, and in fall when the desert broom blooms, you will see pepsis wasps crawling among the branches. They are feeding on the flowers. In their adult stage they are nectar feeders.

But the immature wasps, the larvae, have a very different diet. And there lies the story that fascinates children and adults.

After the wasps mate, it is time for the female to lay her egg. She runs along the ground, darting this way and that, looking for a tarantula burrow. When she finds one she vibrates the silk threads strung out from the burrow entrance. These vibrations tell the tarantula that prey is there. But when it crawls out of the burrow looking for a grasshopper or cricket, there is the wasp instead. The wasp stings the tarantula in the underside of its body. The sting paralyzes the tarantula but does not kill it.

The tarantula quickly becomes helpless and the wasp drags the tarantula to a hole. She pulls the tarantula into the hole, deposits one egg on the abdomen, and seals the opening before she flies away.

A few days later the wasp larva hatches from the egg and there is its fresh food: the living tarantula. As the larva eats, the tarantula finally dies and dries up. But by this time the larva has eaten all it needs. It spins a cocoon and enters the pupa stage. The pupa remains in the burrow through winter, and emerges as an adult in spring.

This fascinating life cycle goes on with other species of wasps, too. Each species of wasp searches out a certain kind of insect or spider that will feed its young. Examples of hosts that are fed on by larval wasps are beetle larvae, mantid eggs, flies, bees, and other wasps.

Adding to this fascinating story is the fact that pepsis wasps are diurnal (active during the day) and tarantulas are nocturnal (active during the night). You may see a pepsis wasp running along the ground in search of a tarantula burrow, but the stinging and dragging to the nest usually takes place in dusk or at night. Also, the tarantula is much larger than the wasp and it must be quite a job to drag the huge load to the nest hole.

Pepsis wasps are not aggressive to humans if they are not handled or molested. But they can give a very painful sting. Have fun observing them, but do not touch!

What are all those bugs swimming in the water?

What fun to find a pool of water on a desert walk! Get down on your hands and knees and spend time observing the little pond. The longer you look, the more creatures you see. Do you see insects swimming along the surface or diving to the bottom? Are there larger creatures lurking in the algae (the green stuff) waiting for prey to come by? Or do you see some other animals that don't quite look like tadpoles, but do not seem to be insects either? Scoop a few into a small container and study them with your hand lens. You will discover a microworld of fascinating creatures. After you have made your observations, return them to the pond.

It is exciting to find water, even if it is only a small puddle collected in a rocky basin. You are most likely to find these surprises in the arroyos or washes during rainy seasons. In winter or early spring, you probably will not find anything swimming in a rain pool — it is too cold. But in summer, when heavy rains fall, one storm after another, pools of water remain for many days. Even large shallow lakes can be found in low plains on lake beds that are normally dry.

Peer into the microhabitat of tiny insects. As they swim about, they feed on material within their watery world: algae, decomposing dead plant and animal material that has fallen in, or other creatures.

The pond may only have existed for a few days, but already there are tiny animals swimming around. Tadpoles come to mind at first (see the question about tadpoles), but there are many other pond dwellers, too; most are insects that require water for part or all of their life spans. Here are a few of the common creatures you are likely to see. How many can you find?

Mosquito Larvae and Pupae

Neither the larva or pupa of a mosquito looks like a mosquito at all. If you see tiny caterpillar-like creatures near the surface of the water which quickly wriggle down to the bottom when you wave your hand over them, you are probably looking at mosquito larvae. They can be found most any time of year in puddles and ponds. They can even be found in tiny pools of water that collect under plant dishes in your yard.

Both larvae and pupae usually are seen suspended just below the surface of the water. Little snorkels extend from their back ends up to the surface, allowing them to breathe. Can you tell a larva from a pupa? The larva is longer and more wiggly. The pupa can swim, too, but it looks like a comma and is not quite as active. They swim by rapidly wriggling their bodies.

Back Swimmers

Back swimmers have six legs as do all insects, but only the two back legs are easily seen. These are long and act as oars, moving the upside down insect through the water. The other four legs are folded down under the head. They swim slightly below the surface of the water preying upon mosquito larva, tadpoles, and other small creatures that swim by. They can breathe under water by using the air trapped in groves on their bodies. They have wings and when the pool dries up they fly to another. Eggs are laid in the water.

Water Boatmen

These insects eat algae and remains of dead debris and are usually found in the mid-depths of the pond. They too have very long back legs that help them swim. They swim right side up.

Water Striders

They can walk on water! How do they do this? Their long legs are covered with hairs which allow them to "skate" on the water surface without sinking. On a sunny day you sometimes can see six bright dots on the bottom of the pond. This is caused by light bending through the places where the feet indent the water surface. They eat insects that land on the surface. The leg hairs help striders feel the water vibrations when something falls into the water.

Giant Water Bug

Among insects it is a giant–about two inches long. The giant water bug is predacious and feeds on anything it can catch, including tadpoles. It has wings and can fly from pond to pond. It can stay underwater a long time and has an abdominal air tube that acts as a snorkel.

Diving Beetles

shiny beetles quickly rising to the surface, then diving ottom. These diving beetles can stay under water a long eath oxygen from a bubble of air they bring down from

Dragonfly and Damselfly Nymphs

The dragonflies and damselflies we see helicoptering in the air, often near water, spend the first part of their lives under water in an immature form called a naiad (NAY ad). Naiads do not look like their parents. They have no wings and blend in well with the algae-covered murky bottoms as they wait for prey. The feed on other pond creatures, especially mosquito larvae. Wiggle your fingers over the pond, or gently prod the bottom with a small twig. You may see a naiad dart out looking for prey. Look around the edges of the pond. You may find the exoskeleton of a dragonfly. This is where a naiad crawled to the edge of the water, molted, and the adult insect flew away. The dry, empty shell remains attached to the pond side, or perhaps on a twig or grass blade protruding from the water. You may see the adults flying near the pool coming in for a drink, or to lay eggs.

Tadpole Shrimp and Fairy Shrimp

Shrimp in the desert? Yes, though it's hard to believe. These tiny crustaceans (hard-shelled animals such as shrimp, lobsters, crabs, and crayfish) seem to magically appear in the ponds created by summer rains. If you see creatures an inch or two in length, tadpole-like in appearance, but with legs that beat with a wavelike movement, you have discovered tadpole shrimp. Fairy shrimp may be seen, too. They are about an inch long and almost transparent. You can see their legs wave as they swim upside down.

Scientists have kept shrimp eggs in dried pond mud in a lab for 15 years, then added water. Out hatched baby shrimp!

How did they get here? The last time a puddle formed here — and this may have been many years ago — the shrimp that swam here mated and the female laid eggs. These hard-shelled eggs dropped to the bottom of the pond. The water evaporated after the rains stopped. Finally the rains fall at the right time and the right place and a pool forms again. The eggs which have survived summer heat, winter cold, and very dry conditions soften and hatch. The young grow, become adults and the life cycle is repeated. Eggs may also be blown about by wind or transported by birds with muddy feet.

The shrimp eat algae, tiny bacteria and protozoa, and gnaw on insect and toad eggs, or dead tadpoles. In turn, they are eaten by predaceous insects, tadpoles, and birds.

Look at the spider web! Where is the spider?

Once you discover spider webs and tune into them, you notice they are everywhere! Examine the different webs you see. Where are they? Look for them woven among shrubs, prickly pear cactus, packrat nests, and over animal burrows. What different shapes can you find? Are any insects trapped in the webs? Can you find the spiders?

One of the most common webs you are likely to see has a funnel shape. The top of the web may be many inches across. The web narrows into a hole in the ground, or into a packrat nest, or into a dense part of a plant, often a prickly pear cactus.

This web was constructed by a funnel-web spider. Flying insects are caught in the upper part of the web. As they wiggle to escape they move downward into the funnel. The spider is waiting at the bottom of the funnel; when it feels the vibrations of the insect on the web, it runs out, grabs the insect, then dashes down into lower part

the web of a funnel-web spider

of the funnel where it eats its meal. If you look into the bottom of a funnel, you might see a spider waiting for its next meal. The funnel-web spider is medium-size, usually brown/gray in color.

The web material starts out as a liquid produced within the spider. This liquid comes out of the spinnerets — those two projections at the back end of the spider's abdomen. When the liquid comes in contact with the air it hardens into strands of silk.

Spider web strands are amazingly strong for their size. Hummingbirds make good use of spider webs in nest building. They weave the strands of web among plant fibers, mosses, and other nest building materials to make a strong nest that stretches to accommodate growing baby hummingbirds.

There are so many species of spiders that it would be impossible to list all the web styles and kinds of spiders here. Just have fun searching for webs and examining the different web patterns. Each species of spider has its own style of web design. Perhaps you can discover a spider hiding somewhere in or near the web. The web is a spider's home as well as it's food trap, so be careful not to destroy a web as you study it.

Spiders generate fear in some people, and myths and horror movies only add to spider phobia. This is a good time for children to get a close look at these fascinating animals, study the interesting webs they make, and talk about how important they are in keeping insect populations in check. This knowledge will engender respect and dispel any fears they may have had.

Will we be attacked by a wild animal?

Which animals do you think may be dangerous: the larger mammals such as coyotes, javelinas, foxes, bobcats, or deer, or smaller animals such as snakes, bees, scorpions, or spiders? Would they have any cause to attack? What can you do to prevent a sting or bite?

A common concern of children who have had limited experience in the natural world is the fear of being chased by a wild animal. Inaccurate portrayals of wildlife in comic books, movies, television (even some of the supposed natural history programs) often characterize animals as vicious hunters out to eat anything in their way. These depictions give children, as well as adults, unwarranted fears of animals. Myths, legends, fables, and children's bedtime stories also exaggerate the fierceness and supernatural attributes of wild animals. It is no wonder some people fear nature.

The truth is wild animals prefer not to have anything to do with us. They hide or run away from people. Most desert animals such as coyotes, bobcats, javelinas, and foxes are not as large as we imagine them to be. They do not want to confront us. But even larger animals should not be feared either. Deer may stop and stare at us a few moments before bounding off. Though mountain lions may be in the area, they are seldom seen. They are nocturnal and very secretive. Black bears live in the higher elevations and are no problem if you take precautions when you are in bear country. Government agencies responsible for trails where there is risk of animal encounters provide safety information for hikers.

Don't reach under rocks, into crevices, and other places you cannot see. In the rare chance a venomous animal is resting there, a rattlesnake could strike, or a scorpion could sting. These would be defensive actions. They aren't about to waste precious venom on something that is not food, but they will bite or sting if they detect potential danger. Bee colonies may be located within crevices along arroyos and occasionally in woodpecker holes in saguaros. If you see bees swarming in and out, stay away. (See the entry **Are there killer bees out here?**)

Stay on the trails. Snakes rest in the shade of plants or rocks and a foot placed nearby could be bitten. These are rare circumstances, but caution is always wise. (See the entry **What do we do if we see a rattle-snake?**)

Do not feed wild animals. Animals are opportunists and will come for food set out by people. This causes them to lose their natural fear of humans and they come closer and closer. People may forget these are still wild animals and move in too close. That is when problems occur. A person is bitten or mauled and the "dangerous wild animal" stories hit the news, fueling fears of nature one more time.

Learn about our wildlife. Fears go away when we understand. Know the precautions to take, too. Then go out and enjoy the wonderful desert trails. If you are observant and quiet you may actually see a wild animal.

Which animal ate that cactus? How can they do that?

Look for signs of animals nibbling on cactuses. Prickly pear often show bite marks. Chollas, and the small hedgehog and pincushion cactuses also may have bite marks.

Examine the bite marks on a prickly pear cactus stem.

Are they curved and rather smooth-edged? Can you see tooth marks? Do the bite marks go around the spines? Can you find clusters of spines that have been dropped to the ground beneath the cactus?

Or...

Are the bitten stems all stringy as if an animal pulled at it with its teeth — spines and all?

If the bite marks you discovered are neatly rounded and show tooth marks, you are looking at the remains of a packrat dinner. At first glance it seems as if a large animal made the large bite. But closer examination reveals that the big bite is the result of many

packrat bites

small bites. The bites go around the spines. Beneath the plant you may see some spines on the ground. They fell there as the packrat chewed around them. The next time you eat a slice of watermelon think about the packrat and the prickly pear. As you eat the watermelon slice you take many, many small bites. After you have finished you have a large, rounded green rind and lots of tooth marks. That's a fairly good illustration of how many small bites end up looking like one large bite. Luckily you do not have to worry about eating around any spines!

If the bite marks you see are all raggedy and stringy, this is probably the result of a javelina's meal. Javelinas aren't dainty about eating and will chomp into prickly pear pads with their big teeth and tear

154

off large pieces — spines and all. If you have a stick of celery in you pack you can illustrate this. Bite down on the celery stalk and then pull the celery from your mouth through your clenched teeth. See how stringy the celery becomes?

Rabbits, squirrels, and some insects also nibble on cactus, but packrat and javelina bites are more commonly seen.

How can animals eat such prickly food? Packrats climb up on a cactus and chew into it. They place their feet in spineless places, or hold on to the spines with their toes. Raw cactus contains kidney-clogging acids that would make us ill, but packrats are able to excrete the acids without damaging their kidneys, a crucial adaptation for animals that include lots of cactus in their diets.

javelina nibbles

Cactus spines do not appear to be a problem to javelinas. Javelinas have tough, leathery mouths which may offer some protection from spines. Spines get stuck in their snouts, but that doesn't deter them from eating more cactus. Spines pass through their digestive systems and can be found intact in their scat. Their kidneys are able to get rid of the cactus acid, too, but they need to drink water to help flush out the acids.

People CAN eat cooked prickly pear. The Spanish word for prickly pear cactus is *nopal*. Prickly pear pads cut into strips and cooked are called *nopalitos*. Most grocery stores have cans or jars of nopalitos in stock. Try them. Eat them as a vegetable or mix in a salad.

Cool Fact!

What if we see a wild pig?

Javelinas, often mistaken for pigs, are common animals of the Sonoran Desert and as you walk the trails you are likely to see them. Javelina signs are easy too find. Look for hoof prints, large, grassy scat, shredded prickly pear cactus, diggings around the bases of plants where roots are exposed and chewed. At any of these signs examine the area closely. You may find long, gray and black stiff hairs which is a clue that javelinas have been around. A musky smell tells you a herd has been nearby recently.

Javelinas, also called collared peccaries, have been the subject of much bad publicity, thus they are feared. They do not attack humans or chase them into trees. It is true that domestic dogs and javelinas often tangle, with the dog coming out on the worse end of the encounter, but that's because dogs get pushy about interfering with the javelinas and their territory. If you see javelinas along the trail, stand back, observe, and enjoy the experience. They won't bother you. They may look your way, sniff the air, then walk off

in another direction. They are nearsighted and rely on their good sense of smell to tell them what's happening in their immediate surroundings.

Though javelinas are more active at night, it is common to see them in the daytime, too, especially in the mornings and early evenings. During the hotter times of day they rest in the shade, often in washes, where the larger trees and cliff sides provide cool, protected places to sleep.

A common misconception is that javelinas are pigs, or oddly, enough, rodents. They are neither. Javelinas are peccaries and belong to their own family, quite different from pigs, and very different from rodents.

They are usually found in herds of six or ten or more. They have young most any time of year and what a treat to see one or two tiny babies walking next to their mother. They are born with eyes open and able to walk. Every javelina has a nipple-like scent gland which exudes a musky odor. The gland is located on the back just above the stubby tail. You may see two javelinas standing next to one another, head to tail, rubbing glands on each other. Each herd of javelinas has its own group scent and this odor keeps the herd together and in communication with one another.

Look at the fuzzy ball walking on the ground. Is it an ant?

Keep your sharp eyes open and you may see a fuzzy insect crawling along the ground. Take a close look, but DO NOT TOUCH! What color is the "fuzz" on the abdomen (the back section): orange-red, yellow, or white? Stand still and watch it walk along. It sure looks like an ant, but it isn't. What, then, could it be?

You have discovered a velvet ant. Though it may appear to be an ant, it's really a wasp. These colorful insects catch your eye as they scurry over the soil and among the rocks. Some species may be an inch in length. There are a number of species, but the velvet ant you are most likely to see has a large abdomen covered with orange-red hairs and black hairs covering the head and thorax.

Other species have yellow or red abdomens. There is a smaller velvet ant that has white hair and looks like a creosote bush seed with legs. The hair-like coat is really made of bristles called setae (singular is seta) which are projections of the cuticle. Your hair, mammalian hair, grows out of glands called follicles. The insect you see probably does not have wings. That means it is a female. Males are winged and are not seen as often as females. It may be tempting to pick up a fuzzy velvet ant, but never do it. It is the female wasp and bee that has the stinger. Velvet ants have very long stingers and can give a powerful sting. Adult velvet ants feed on nectar, fruit, and other sweet foods.

Cool Fact!

As is true of most wasps, the larvae are parasites on other arthropods. The female finds a nest of a burrowing insect, often that of a burrowing bee. She lays an egg on the larva or pupa and leaves. When the velvet ant egg hatches the larva eats the host larva or pupa. It then pupates and later emerges from the burrow as an adult wasp.

Eeeeew! Animal poop!

Animal droppings, called scat, are often seen on the trail. Scat and urine may be deposited at definite sites to proclaim territory. Rather than looking at them in disgust, look at them as a natural part of a walk in the outdoors. You can even learn from them. The droppings will tell you which animal came by and what it had to eat. Luckily, desert animals usually leave very dry scat. Take a few sticks and poke apart the scat. What do you find? Do you see hair or fur? Tiny bones? Seeds? Grassy material? What is the shape and size of the scat? Where did you find it? These are clues to help you answer the question, "Whose scat is that?".

Desert Tortoise Scat
SIZE 1 inch (2.5 cm) or more
SHAPE long oval
MATERIAL packed with grass and other plant material
COLOR fresh scat may be greenish, dried scat is gray
OTHER look beneath animal burrows along the sides of arroyos

Bobcat Scat
SIZE up to 4 inches (10 cm) long
SHAPE similar to coyote scat but often segmented by constrictions
    (like a Tootsie Roll)
MATERIAL fur and bones, never plant matter
OTHER cats try to cover their scat, so look for scratch marks and
    a mound of dirt

Mule Deer Scat
SIZE about ¾ inch (1.9 cm) long
SHAPE oval; almost round
COLOR dark brown
OTHER individual scats are small, but there are usually many
    in a small area

Coyote Scat

SIZE varies, depending upon the food the coyote has eaten,
and may be 4 inches (10 cm) long
SHAPE long oval, often with a long "tail" at one end
MATERIAL scat is mostly hair and bone fragments; when saguaro
and prickly pear cactus fruit are ripe, scat contains mostly seeds
COLOR usually gray
OTHER commonly found along trails

Domestic dog scat may also be found along the trails, but you can tell the difference between dog and coyote scat. Dog droppings are consistent in color and texture; coyote scat isn't and may include hair and bone.

Javelina Scat

SIZE up to 2−3 three inches (5−7.5 cm) in length
SHAPE long oval
MATERIAL grass, seeds, leaves
COLOR gray, tan, may be greenish if fresh

Cottontail Rabbit and Jackrabbit Scat

SIZE   less than ½ inch (1.2 cm) across
SHAPE nearly a perfect sphere
MATERIAL grass and other plant material
COLOR   usually a yellow-tan

Packrat (Wood Rat) Scat

SIZE ½ inch (1.2 cm) long
SHAPE long oval
COLOR black
OTHER found around stick nests and arroyo burrows

Horned Lizard Scat

SIZE up to 1 inch (2.5 cm) long
SHAPE long oval
MATERIAL consists entirely of ant bodies packed together
COLOR black

	Scat*	Tracks*
Desert Tortoise		
Bobcat		
Mule deer		
Coyote		
Javelina		
Cottontail		
Packrat		
Horned lizard		

*scat and tracks not to scale

Is that a chipmunk (or prairie dog)?

Is it really a chipmunk? or prairie dog? Put your observations skills to use. Note the markings. Do you see stripes? Where are the stripes located on the animal's body? What is the size of the animal?

If you are in the desert you will NOT see a chipmunk or a prairie dog. Those are not desert animals. The animal you see is one of the ground squirrels. Two common desert ground squirrels are often mistaken for the non-desert rodents. Here are some comparisons to help you remember which rodent is which.

Harris' antelope ground squirrel
- lives in the desert
- a single white stripe along each side goes from the shoulder to base of the tail
- no stripes on the head
- face is not pointed
- small ears are set close to the head
- bushy tail is often arched over the back

Cliff chipmunk (Arizona species)
- lives in nearby mountains and down into lower elevations among scrub oak and manzanita
- stripes are on the on back and not well defined
- three brown and two white stripes go from nose to ears
- pointed face
- ears stand out from head
- long, bushy tail; usually not arched over the back

Round-tailed ground squirrel

- lives in the desert
- 3 inch (7.6cm) long black-tipped tail; not bushy
- weighs 6–7 ounces (170–198 grams); slender
- 9 inches (22.8cm) long
- tan; lighter underneath

Prairie dog

- lives in grasslands (whitetail prairie dogs live in northeastern Arizona; blacktail prairie dogs once lived in southeastern Arizona grasslands but were exterminated by ranchers)
- short tail (same length as hind foot), not bushy
- weighs 1.5–2.5 pounds (.68–1.13 kg); pudgy
- 12 inches (30.4 cm) long
- yellowish

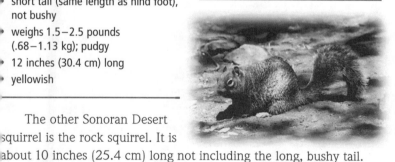

The other Sonoran Desert squirrel is the rock squirrel. It is about 10 inches (25.4 cm) long not including the long, bushy tail.

Enjoy watching the squirrels run about gathering food. You may see a ground squirrel climb an ocotillo and munch on the flowers high on a branch tip, or climb a prickly pear cactus or barrel cactus to eat the fruit and seeds. Or you may see one standing tall on its hind legs watchful for danger.

Of the three Sonoran Desert squirrels, only the Harris' antelope squirrel can be seen all year. The round-tailed ground squirrel hibernates in winter and the rock squirrel retreats to its burrow during cold periods. To announce territory, especially during the spring mating season, squirrels give high pitched shrill whistles that can be mistaken for bird calls.

Cool Fact!

163

If we find an animal, can I take it home to keep it as pet?

You make a wonderful discovery along the trail: a desert tortoise, a horned lizard, a tarantula, or perhaps a baby bird or mammal. Wouldn't it make a cool pet? Or would it? Could it survive in your yard? What would you feed it? What is its life span? (Some animals live many years and you would have a very long-term commitment to care for the animal.) Would you be breaking the law by taking it home? There are many factors to consider.

Children are enamored with the idea of having a wild animal pet — it would be so different from a dog or cat. Friends would love to come over to play with it, and it would be fun to show off an unusual pet. But would there be problems feeding and housing the animal? Equally important, what problems would the animal have after being taken from its home? Following are suggestions for discussions you and your children can have concerning practicality and ethics of wild animal "pets."

Just as you feel safe and comfortable in your home, a wild animal feels secure in its territory. There it can find food and shelter from weather or predators. Many animals will not survive if taken from their homes. They will not eat and therefore will die.

Feeding wild animals is not like feeding a dog or cat; many have special dietary needs. Tarantulas need live insects. Tortoises feed on plant material containing certain nutrients—lettuce is not enough. Snakes need mice. Horned lizards need a fresh and constant supply of certain species of ants. These foods aren't neatly packaged in the grocery store.

As tempting as it may be, never remove an animal from the wild. Each and every one plays an important role within its habitat.
- Many insects and birds pollinate flowers.
- Many animals scatter seeds.
- Rodents and other animals dig holes which aerate the soil.
- Some birds, lizards, all spiders, and even insects eat insects.
- Many birds, mammals, and snakes eat rodents.
- Prey species are food for other animals.
- The predator/prey relationship is vital to keep populations in check.

Many wild animals cannot be toilet trained. Need we say more?

Many mammals, especially desert mammals are nocturnal. While you are awake the animal is sleeping. While you are trying to sleep the animal is active and keeping you awake.

Baby mammals and birds look so cute and you may be able to handle them when young, but when they reach adulthood their wild instincts develop, too. Mammals bite and scratch, birds peck and claw. They become too difficult and dangerous to handle.

Many animals live a very long time. Female tarantulas live about 20 years. Tortoises live 50 or more years. That's a long time to care for an animal. Once an animal is removed from the wild it is gone from the wild forever. An animal is probably doomed when people make the unfortunate choice of taking it from its natural environ-ment, then deciding to put it back in the wild when they tire of it. It is unable to find food or shelter in an unfamiliar habitat, or it may have lost its natural ability to find food or shelter and it becomes easy prey for other animals. The area may already be occupied by another animal of the same species which will fight for its territory.

Perhaps the released animal carries a disease which could spread to the wild animal populations.

Many people mistakenly think baby animals that are alone have been abandoned. This is seldom the case. Usually the mother is nearby. A baby animal, if taken from its home, will most certainly die. Only the parents of baby birds or mammals can do the best job of feeding their babies.

There are so many interrelationships between living things and the environment that we may not know what effects there may be by removing animals from their native habitats.

Then there are the legal problems. If you are on county, state, or federal land, you are not allowed to take anything away. Even on private property there are laws about collecting some animals. Most species of birds and mammals are protected. Desert tortoises and some species of snakes and lizards are protected, too. Insects, spiders, and other arthropods do not have legal protection on private land, but they, too, should be allowed to remain in their homes. And the rights of private land owners should always be respected.

Why these laws? The wild animals are an important part of the environment. Their interrelationships with the other animals, plants, even the non-living parts of the environment form a "web" of connections. If some people decided to collect all the tortoises, for example, and sell them as pets, a piece of that web would be missing and many other animals and plants would be affected. You may think, "Oh, what does one tortoise matter?" But it does.

So it's a good thing these laws exist. They are reminders that taking animals from the wild is never a good idea.

You may ask, "What about zoos?" Good question. Most zoo animals are born in captivity and could never be released to the wild. Some were injured when they were hit by cars, shot at, or harmed by other unfortunate events. Others were "pets" that people could no longer manage. These animals are fed and cared for by professional animal keepers. Zoos also serve an important role in educating us about natural history.

The best way to appreciate our wild animals is to observe them in their wild, natural homes.

Family Trails
in Tucson
and Phoenix

It's a magical world, Hobbes, Ol' Buddy...
let's go exploring!

Calvin's last words,
December 31, 1995
(Calvin & Hobbes)

here can you go for a family walk and learn about our desert? You will find easy access to trails no matter where you live. In this section is a brief description of trails for your family to explore. Some are within the urban area, others are a short distance from town. The trails are suitable for everyone, even the small members of your family. Do not be intimidated by the longer trails; you do not have to walk the full length. Walk as far as you wish, then turn around and retrace your steps — you will not get bored with the scenery. But turn around before you are too tired. Remember, you must walk an equal distance back to the start of the trail.

More complete descriptions of many of these trails can be found in hiking guides found in local bookstores. See the Suggested Reading section for titles. Detailed maps are also available from various agencies.

Scout around for other places to walk, too. Perhaps there are neighborhood parks and open areas near your home that offer desert landscapes.

On the following pages are descriptions and information on trails in the Tucson and Phoenix areas.

Tucson

WEST

Arizona-Sonora Desert Museum

Tucson Mountain Park
- Brown Mountain
- David Yetman Trail

Feliz Paseos Universally Accessible Park

Greasewood Park

Saguaro National Park, West District
- King Canyon
- Signal Hill
- Cactus Garden
- Desert Discovery Trail
- Valley View Overlook
- Sweetwater Trail
- Thunderbird Trail

Pima Community College, West Campus

EAST

Saguaro National Park, East District
- Visitor Center Interpretive Trail
- Desert Ecology Trail
- Freeman Homestead Nature Trail
- Tanque Verde Ridge Trail
- Cactus Forest Trail

Case Park

NORTHWEST

Arthur Pack Regional Park

Cañada del Oro Riverfront Park

Catalina State Park
- Romero Ruins Trail
- Nature Trail
- Birding Trail

Pima Canyon

Tohono Chul Park

NORTHEAST

Sabino Canyon
- Bajada Loop Nature Trail
- Tramside walks

Agua Caliente Park

Catalina Foothills High School/ Sky Club Wash Natural Area

SOUTHEAST

Lincoln Park

SOUTHWEST

John F. Kennedy Park Regional Park

CENTRAL

Tucson Botanical Gardens

WEST

ARIZONA-SONORA DESERT MUSEUM

Area	Tucson Mountains
Agency/Org	Arizona-Sonora Desert Museum
Fee	Entrance fee, children under six are free. Memberships available.
Directions	West on Speedway, over Gates Pass, to Kinney Road. Turn right and follow signs to Arizona Sonora Desert Museum.
Facilities	Restrooms, drinking fountains, lunch room and restaurant.
Note	Almost 2 miles of paths are located within the Museum grounds. All are wheelchair accessible. The Desert Loop trail is featured here because it allows for a more intimate desert experience. The unpaved trail winds through natural desert, and is some distance from the busier, more formal exhibit areas.

Trail	**DESERT LOOP TRAIL**
Difficulty	Easy, wheelchair accessible
Length	.5 mile loop
Trail Details	Unpaved, level trail. Exhibits of animals in natural habitats along the way.
Features	The trail winds among typical Arizona Upland desert vegetation. Visitors have excellent views of coyotes and javelinas wandering or sleeping just behind the almost invisible fencing alongside the trail. More exhibits are in progress. To the west are sweeping views of Avra and Altar Valleys and the mountain ranges beyond.

TUCSON MOUNTAIN PARK

Area	Tucson Mountains
Agency/Org	Tucson Mountain Park
	Pima County Parks and Recreation
Fee	None
Restrictions	No dogs are allowed on Tucson Mountain Park trails

Trail	**BROWN MOUNTAIN**
Directions	West on Speedway, over Gates Pass, to Kinney Road. Turn right and follow signs to Arizona Sonora Desert Museum. Drive 2.3 miles to the Juan Santa Cruz picnic area. It is on the left just before the Desert Museum. A parking area is left of the trailhead sign.
Facilities	Picnic benches and pit toilets at Juan Santa Cruz picnic area.
Difficulty	Moderate
Length	The entire loop is 5 miles, but walk as far as you wish, then retrace steps back to the parking area.
Trail Details	The trailhead is at the far west end of the picnic area. Look for the trailhead sign and the stairs into the drainage. The trail ascends upwards to the top of the ridge and continues along the ridge top, alternating from east to west of the ridgetop.
Features	Good views of Avra Valley to the west, the Arizona-Sonora Desert Museum to the northwest, and the Tucson Mountains to the east and south. Good examples of different vegetation types on southwest and northeast facing slopes.

Trail	**DAVID YETMAN TRAIL**
Directions	West on Speedway to Camino de Oeste, 3.7 miles from Silverbell Road. (A short distance from the Speedway/Anklam Road intersection Speedway becomes Gates Pass Road.) Look for Camino de Oeste. Turn left (south) on Camino de Oeste and drive .7 miles on unpaved road to the parking area. If you wish to walk the entire trail (5.4 miles) you will need to shuttle cars. Leave one car at the Camino de Oeste trailhead and another car at the parking area at the bottom of Gates Pass Road at the Scenic View Pullout G3. Look to the east and up the old jeep trail for the David Yetman Trailhead sign.
Facilities	None
Difficulty	Moderate to somewhat difficult. The easier route is Gates Pass to Camino de Oeste, however the first few hundred yards of the trail are rocky and steep.
Length	One-way, from Gates Pass trailhead to the Camino de Oeste trailhead is 5.4 miles. If you do not wish to shuttle cars, or that distance is too long, walk the first part of the trail from either trailhead and walk as far as you wish.
Trail Details	If you are walking only a part of the trail, the Camino de Oeste end is suggested. It is closer to Tucson and the features are quite varied. This is the section of trail described here.

The trailhead is at the south end of the parking area. If you are walking the entire trail, begin from the Gates Pass trailhead and walk to Camino de Oeste. This route is easier with less elevation gain.

Features   The first part of the trail leading from the Camino de Oeste trailhead goes through a wide wash. Trees and shrubs such as mesquite, desert hackberry, and catclaw acacia grow along the wash. Superb stands of saguaros cover the rocky hillsides; good examples of lichen can be found on the boulders. About a mile in the trail climbs out of the wash to the ruins of a rock house, built in the 1930s and occupied for a number of years by the Bowen family. Walk as far as you wish and retrace your steps back to the car.

Cautions   Mountain bikes and horses share the trail with hikers.

FELIZ PASEOS UNIVERSALLY ACCESSIBLE PARK

This park is in the process of being developed as a Universally Accessible Park. Projected opening of the park is Spring 2001.

Area   Tucson Mountains

Agency/Org Pima County Parks and Recreation

Fee   None

Address   1600 N. Camino de Oeste

Directions   Drive west on Speedway. Turn right onto Camino de Oeste. The park is on the east side of the road 1/4 mile north of West Speedway.

Facilities   Fully accessible parking area, restrooms, water fountains, emergency telephone, and picnic facilities are built to ADA (American with Disabilities Act) code.

Features   This is Pima County's first fully designed universally accessible park, offering people of all levels of ability an intimate experience with the natural landscape. Most paths are designed for wheelchairs and strollers and additional trails offer more challenging terrain. A trail access sign gives information on each trail so visitors can choose routes best suited for them. Several miles of trails wind through pristine desert landscape at the foot of the Tucson Mountains. This is truly a park for everyone.

GREASEWOOD PARK

Area	Tucson Mountain foothills
Agency/Org	Tucson Parks and Recreation Department
Fee	None
Address	1075 N. Greasewood Road
Directions	West on Speedway, turn left (south) on Greasewood Road. Park entrance is immediately to the right (west).
Facilities	Pit toilets, drinking fountain, picnic benches, cooking grills, group ramada

Trail	**NATURE TRAIL AND WILDERNESS TRAIL**
Difficulty	Easy
Length	Nature trail is a paved walkway a few hundred yards. Wilderness Trail is dirt and leads in various directions. Walk as far as you wish.
Trail Details	Trailhead information at end of parking area. Paved area is wheelchair accessible. Dirt trails meander through desert and Anklam Wash.
Features	This is the first natural desert park set aside by the City of Tucson. In many areas along the trails the encroaching urban suburbs cannot be seen. Engraved stone markers identify plants along the paved Nature Trail. The Wilderness Trail winds through typical palo verde/saguaro upland community and dips into Anklam Wash. Walk along the wash and note the different vegetation. Packrat burrows are common in the cliffsides.

SAGUARO NATIONAL PARK, WEST DISTRICT

Area	Tucson Mountains
Agency/Org	Saguaro National Park, West District
Fee	No entrance fee to the West District
Trail map	Obtain the free "Trails in the Tucson Mountain District" map at the Visitor Center.

Trail	**KING CANYON**
Directions	West on Speedway, over Gates Pass, to Kinney Road. Turn right and follow signs to Arizona-Sonora Desert Museum. Go .1 mile beyond Museum entrance. Parking area is on the right.
Facilities	Picnic benches, ramadas, pit toilet at Mam-a-Gah picnic area one mile from trailhead.

Difficulty	Moderate. Slow rise in elevation along the trail. Some drops from rock ledges along canyon bottom.
Length	2 miles roundtrip.
Trail Details	The trail begins on the north side of the parking area. Follow the trail for about a mile. It drops into the canyon near the Mam-a-Gah picnic shelter. Return by walking down the canyon bottom. As you approach Kinney Road, look to your left for the trail that leads back up to the parking area.
Features	The higher trail and the wash bottom offer good contrasts to the different vegetation found in each habitat. After a good winter rainy season the hillside is covered with many species of spring flowers. Look for ferns and sellaginella in shady areas. A permanent spring is located in the area where you enter the wash. Unless it has been extremely dry, there will be pools in rocky basins along the wash. Look for water insects and tadpoles in summer. Footprints of coyote, deer, javelina, and other wildlife are often at the water's edge. Soon after you enter the canyon look for petroglyphs on both sides of the rock walls. These were etched by the Hohokam 900 to 1300 A.D.

Trail	**SIGNAL HILL PETROGLYPH TRAIL**
Directions	West on Speedway, over Gates Pass, to Kinney Road. Turn right, pass the Arizona-Sonora Desert Museum and continue to Saguaro National Park. Pass the Visitor Center. Kinney Road intersects with Sandario Road. Turn right on Sandario Road, then right onto Golden Gate Road. Drive 1.5 miles to Signal Hill Picnic area.
Facilities	Picnic benches, ramadas, pit toilets
Difficulty	Moderate. Short climb to the hilltop.
Length	.25 mile
Trail Details	The trail begins north of the picnic area. A short climb winds to the top of the hill.
Features	Excellent Hohokam petroglyphs are abundant on the boulders. This vantage point offers good views of the surrounding desert, the Tucson Mountains, and Avra Valley.

Trail	**CACTUS GARDEN TRAIL**
Directions	West on Speedway, over Gates Pass, to Kinney Road. Turn right, pass the Arizona-Sonora Desert Museum and continue to Saguaro National Park Visitor Center parking.
Facilities	Restrooms and drinking fountains at the Visitor Center.

Difficulty	Easy. Wheelchair accessible.
Length	100 yards.
Trail Details	The trail begins left of the parking lot.
Features	Interpretive signs along the trail describe desert plant adaptations. An additional short loop takes you down to the Javelina Wash Trail. Good examples of animal burrows are found in the gravel banks. The Visitor Center has displays, a slide program, and bookshop.

Trail	**DESERT DISCOVERY TRAIL**
Directions	West on Speedway, over Gates Pass, to Kinney Road. Turn right, pass the Arizona-Sonora Desert Museum and continue to Saguaro National Park. Pass the Visitor Center and drive one mile. Trail is on the west side of the road.
Facilities	No water or toilet facilities. There are many shade ramadas and benches along the trail.
Difficulty	Easy. Wheelchair accessible.
Length	.5 mile loop.
Trail Details	Trailhead starts from parking area.
Features	Signs along the trail interpret desert animal and plant life.

Trail	**VALLEY VIEW OVERLOOK**
Directions	West on Speedway, over Gates Pass, to Kinney Road. Turn right, pass the Arizona-Sonora Desert Museum and continue to Saguaro National Park. Pass the Visitor Center and drive for 1.6 miles. Turn right (east) onto Hohokam Road. Drive 1.5 miles to Valley View Overlook Trail parking area on left (west) of road
Facilities	None. Picnic benches and pit toilets at nearby Sus picnic area.
Difficulty	Moderate.
Length	1.5 miles round trip.
Trail Details	Trail passes through two washes and gradually ascends to a ridge.
Features	Good stands of ironwood trees. Excellent views of Avra Valley to the west and Picacho Peak to the north.

Trail	**SWEETWATER TRAIL**
Directions	From Silverbell Road turn west on El Camino del Cerro. Drive 5 miles to the El Camino del Cerro trailhead parking area.
Facilities	None

Difficulty	Moderate
Length	Depends upon your group. You may walk a short way and retrace your steps, or you may continue to the top of Wasson Peak (4.6 miles to Wasson trail) with steep climbs or connecting trails from King Canyon or Hugh Norris.
Trail Details	Rocky trail with changes in elevation throughout.
Features	Excellent examples of Tucson Mountain foothill vegetation.

Trail	**THUNDERBIRD TRAIL**
Directions	From Silverbell Road turn west on El Camino del Cerro. Drive 5 miles to the Camino del Cerro trailhead parking area.
Facilities	None
Difficulty	Moderate
Length	1.8 miles roundtrip to Park boundary. Trail continues east from there.
Trail Details	Trailhead is west of the parking lot. Walk .2 miles to the Thunderbird Trail sign. Turn right. The trail goes along the Saguaro National Park boundary line. Rocky trail with minor changes in elevation.
Features	Excellent examples of Tucson Mountain foothill vegetation. CAUTION: There are open mine shafts along this trail and other trails in the Tucson Mountains. They are fenced off and marked with warning signs, but they are deep and curious hikers have been known to fall in.

PIMA COMMUNITY COLLEGE, WEST CAMPUS

Area	Tucson Mountain foothills
Agency/Org	Pima Community College
Fee	None

Trail	**CAMPUS TRAILS**
Directions	West on Speedway, turn left (south) on Greasewood Road. Look to your left and enter Pima Community College entrance road. Veer to the left and park near the recreational facilities (tennis courts, track, etc.).
Facilities	None
Difficulty	Easy
Length	Trails crisscross the natural desert. Walk a few yards or a few miles.
Trail Details	Walk around the west of the fenced track to the trail which

leads from the north side of the track area. Walk in any direction. A number of trails intersect; any trail is good.

Features   In this half square mile excellent natural desert is preserved among encroaching development; but even with housing on two sides and Pima Community College on another, a wide variety of birdlife is abundant, and javelina and coyotes are often seen.

EAST

SAGUARO NATIONAL PARK - EAST DISTRICT

Area	Rincon Mountains
Agency/Org	Saguaro National Park, East Unit
Fee	Fee per car load; or fee for an annual pass
Directions	Drive east on Broadway or 22nd Street then right on Houghton Road and left on Old Spanish Trail Road. The park entrance is on the left.
Trail Map	Obtain the free "Day Hiking Trails of the Rincon Mountain District" map at the Visitor Center.

Trail	**VISITOR CENTER INTERPRETIVE TRAIL**
Difficulty	Easy. Wheelchair accessible
Length	.1 mile
Directions	The interpretive trail is located immediately west of the Visitor Center.
Facilities	Benches, ramada, drinking fountain, and toilets are available nearby. Bookstore, interpretive displays, and audio visual programs are available in the Visitor Center.

Trail	**DESERT ECOLOGY TRAIL**
Directions	Drive 2.4 miles past the entrance station on Cactus Forest Drive.
Facilities	None
Difficulty	Easy. Wheelchair accessible
Length	.25 mile
Trail Details	The trailhead is across the street from the parking area. Benches are located along the trail.
Features	Interpretive signs emphasize role of water in the desert.

Trail	**FREEMAN HOMESTEAD NATURE TRAIL**
Directions	The trailhead is on Cactus Forest Drive about 1 mile south of the entrance station.
Facilities	Covered picnic benches and pit toilets at nearby Javelina picnic area.
Difficulty	Easy
Length	1 mile.
Trail Details	Loop trail near Javelina picnic area
Features	Interpretive signs discuss homesteading in the Tucson basin.

Trail	**TANQUE VERDE RIDGE TRAIL**
Directions	The trailhead is past the entrance station on Cactus Forest Drive about 1 mile south, near the Javelina picnic area.
Facilities	Picnic tables and pit toilets at nearby Javelina picnic area.
Difficulty	Moderate to difficult depending upon length of walk.
Length	The length of your walk depends on the abilities of your group. The trail goes to the higher elevations and backcountry of the Rincon Mountains.
Trail Details	Trail begins to the right of Javelina picnic area. A sign indicates parking for trail hikers.
Features	The beginning of the trail crosses small arroyos. The trail reaches Tanque Verde Ridge 1.5 miles in; it then follows the ridge line. There are excellent views of Tucson and surrounding mountain ranges. As you continue the gentle climb you notice changes in vegetation. Typical desert plants are less common and higher elevation plants such as juniper and grasses appear.

Trail	**CACTUS FOREST TRAIL**
Directions	This trail transverses the western end of the Park; it can be accessed from a number of trailheads. Trailheads can be accessed from Broadway Blvd. and Old Spanish Trail. Two other trailheads are along the Cactus Forest Drive. See the park map for details.
Difficulty	Easy
Length	5.2 miles one way. The trail crosses the west side of the park. Walk as far as you wish and return to the parking area, or park cars at each end of the trail and shuttle.
Trail Details	A flat, sandy trail.
Facilities	None
Features	The trail winds among old growth saguaros.

CASE DISTRICT PARK

Area	East
Agency/Org	Tucson Parks and Recreation Department
Fee	None
Address	9851 E. Kenyon Drive
Directions	Drive east on 22nd Street. Pass Old Spanish Trail and turn left on Bonanza Avenue. Turn right (east) onto Kenyon Drive to the park.
Facilities	Parking lot, playground equipment, interpretive signs.

Trail	**(Trails under development)**
Difficulty	Easy
Trail Details	Trails are being developed; they will be accessible to wheelchairs and strollers.
Features	This is Tucson Park and Recreation Department's first natural resource park. Recreation opportunities come from the natural surroundings and consist of a desert trail, interpretive signs, and playground equipment set among the desert landscape. The park, surrounded by subdivisions, was set aside as a natural retreat by Leland D. Case who donated a portion of the land. The City of Tucson bought additional land bringing the total area to 50 acres.

NORTHWEST

ARTHUR PACK REGIONAL PARK

Area	Northwest: Thornydale Road and Hardy Road
Agency/Org	Pima County Parks and Recreation Department
Fee	None
Address	Hardy Road
Directions	Drive north on Thornydale Road. One half mile north of Cortaro Farms Road turn left (west) on Hardy Road. The road dead ends in .5 miles. Park along Hardy Road or in the Tortolita Middle School parking lot.
Facilities	None

Trail	**NATURE TRAIL**
Difficulty	Easy
Length	A mile or two depending on which trail you take. The natural area is approximately one square mile.
Trail Details	Look for the opening along the fence line on the north side of the street. A few signs give regulations about the soccer field to the right. There are no signs designating the trail. Turn to your left as you enter the gate and you are on the trail.
Features	Flat, mostly sandy trails meander and criss-cross throughout the area. Walk up Hardy Wash. Look for birds in the huge ironwood and palo verde trees. Huge saguaros are many-armed and riddled with woodpecker holes. During fall and winter birds, notably phainopeplas, feed from the huge mistle-toes hanging in the trees. Packrat nest are common, and their feeding on cactus is evident. Many saguaro trunks are girdled and prickly pear and chollas are nibbled by the chewing rodents.
Cautions	ATVs may be on trails.

CAÑADA DEL ORO RIVERFRONT PARK

Area	Northwest
Agency/Org	Oro Valley Parks and Recreation
Fee	None
Address	551 West Lambert Lane
Directions	North on La Cañada Drive, turn east on Lambert Lane. Drive 1.1 miles. The entrance is on the south side. Or drive north on Oracle; turn left on First Avenue; turn left on Lambert Lane. Drive 1.2 miles. Entrance is on the south side.
Facilities	Restrooms, picnic ramadas, concession building, a children's play area, and a grassy amphitheater and performance area.

This is the first park built by the town of Oro Valley. The perimeter of the park remains natural desert. There are no desert trails within the park, but there is free access to Cañada del Oro wash on the south side of the park.

Trail	**CAÑADA DEL ORO WASH**
	Look for an opening in the fence south of the soccer field. There is no trail, but continue south for a short distance and you are in the sandy wash.
Difficulty	Easy, flat, sandy wash bottom. Not satisfactory for strollers or wheelchairs.

Length	The length of your walk is up to you. You may walk the wash in either direction then retrace your steps back to the starting point. (Cañada del Oro wash begins in the Santa Catalina Mountains to the north and continues south to the Rillito River.)
Features	The sandy soil and water runoff from the Santa Catalinas provide a good habitat for desert broom, desert willow, catclaw acacias, and mesquites which grow to unusual heights along the sides of the wash. A large population of Gambel's quail, cottontail rabbits, and lizards scurry about under the dense growth. Many birds can be seen and heard in the trees and brush.
Cautions	The trail is Cañada del Oro wash and is unimproved. Do not walk in the wash during summer rains or heavy winter rains. Runoff from the mountains creates a deep, fast moving river. Be alert for ATV's (all-terrain vehicles) in the wash.

CATALINA STATE PARK

Area	Northwest. Western foothills of the Catalina Mountains.
Agency/Org	Arizona State Parks
Fee	Entrance fee. Free trails map.
Directions	Drive north on State Highway 77 (Oracle Road). The park entrance is on the right (east) at mile marker 81, six miles north of Ina Road.
Facilities	Pit toilets, picnic areas

Trail	**ROMERO RUIN TRAIL**
Difficulty	Moderate; benches along the trail
Length	.33 mile; loop trail
Trail Details	Look for the trailhead sign on the main park road near the picnic area. Parking is to the left of the road. Trail starts to the right of the road. Steps lead to the top of the hill. Loop trail on the hill top is level.
Features	This is the site of a Hohokam village. The Hohokam were prehistoric desert Indians who occupied a large area within the Sonoran Desert. Interpretive signs tell about Hohokam life and how they survived on desert foods. Only a few rows of stones indicate the village walls. Tall cholla cacti holding bird nests are common along the trail. Good view of Catalina Mountains and surrounding desert from the hilltop.

Trail	**NATURE TRAIL**
Difficulty	Moderate; benches along the trail
Length	1 mile; loop trail
Trail Details	Drive to the end of the paved road. Parking is on the left. The trailhead begins at the end of the road turnaround. The first part of the trail is a steep climb; the loop at the top of the hill is flat.
Features	Signs along the loop trail give general interpretations of geology of the region, desert adaptations of plants and animals. Other signs give facts about some common animals, along with their footprints imbedded in cement pads. Granite boulders sparkle. Mesquite, grasses, and cholla cactus are the dominant plants. Good views of surrounding desert.

Trail	**BIRDING TRAIL**
Difficulty	Moderate; benches along the trail
Length	1 mile; loop trail
Trail Details	Drive to the end of the paved road; parking is on the left. The trailhead begins across the road from the parking area. The first part of the trail involves a climb up a number of steps. The section at the top of the hill is flat.
Features	Signs along the trail address the three different types of habitat found on this walk. You'll see some oak trees supporting mistletoe. This is the leafier mistletoe, unlike the twiggy desert mistletoe found on mesquites, and acacias. Look toward the Catalinas for excellent examples of vegetation differences between north-facing and south-facing slopes. Northern exposures are covered with sotol and hopbush, plants which require cooler temperatures. South facing exposures are prime saguaro habitat.

PIMA CANYON

Area	Northwest
Agency/Org	Pima County Parks and Recreation (trailhead parking) Coronado National Forest (trail)
Fee	None
Directions	Drive north on Oracle Road to Magee Road (1 mile north of Ina), then east on Magee Road for 1.6 miles to the trail-head parking.
Facilities	None

Trail	PIMA CANYON
Difficulty	Moderate to somewhat strenuous. Some steep rocky steps.
Length	The first 3 miles are moderate; the trail then becomes difficult as it continues upward to Pusch Ridge for a total of 7 miles, one way.
Trail Details	Walk this trail only after the members of your group are able to climb some steep rocky sections of trail. It is not very difficult, but would not be wise for a beginning or very young hiker. The first half mile trail goes through private land. A gate and signs indicate entrance to Coronado National Forest.
Features	To the north the steep mountain side above the trail is studded with tall saguaros. Look for raptors perched on saguaros or soaring above the cliffs. To the south, the streambed is visible. To the south and west Tucson spreads out across the valley. After about a mile the trail drops to the canyon floor and continues alongside the stream bed. Within a half mile you are treated to welcome shade as you walk beneath a grove of cottonwood trees. The trail follows the canyon floor for 2 miles then climbs to a rock dam, a source of water for wildlife. The dam is 3 miles from the parking area.

TOHONO CHUL PARK

Area	Ina Road and Oracle Road
Agency/Org	Tohono Chul Park (non-profit organization)
Fee	Donations accepted. Annual membership available.
Address	7366 North Paseo del Norte
Directions	One block west of Oracle Road, on Ina Road, turn north at the stoplight. Park entrance is on the right (east).
Facilities	Restrooms, restaurant, two gift shops, demonstration garden, plant sale greenhouse.

Trail	NATURE TRAILS, NORTH AND SOUTH LOOPS
Difficulty	Easy, wheelchair accessible
Length	A .75 mile south trail and a .25 mile north trail.
Trail Details	Trail map and self-guiding tour booklet available. Park encompasses 37 acres.
Features	The south trail winds through gardens, exhibits, and washes. The north trail winds through natural desert. Several pools on the grounds attract wildlife. Good birdwatching throughout the park.

NORTHEAST

SABINO CANYON RECREATION AREA

Area	Northeast
Agency/Org	Coronado National Forest
Fee	Call for current fee information: (520) 670-4552
Address	5700 North Sabino Canyon Road
Directions	From Tanque Verde Road turn north and drive 4.5 miles on Sabino Canyon Road to the Visitor Center.
Facilities	Restrooms, water fountains, picnic areas, information center, gift shop, tram rides (fee).

There are many trails of varying lengths and difficulty throughout the Recreation Area. Following are a few suggestions.

Trail	**BAJADA LOOP NATURE TRAIL**
Difficulty	Easy, wheelchair accessible
Length	.5 mile
Trail Details	Near the Visitor Center; flat, dirt trail.
Features	Trail winds through typical desert vegetation. Signs identify plants.

Trail	**SABINO CANYON**
Difficulty	Easy to moderate depending upon length of your walk. Total elevation gain is 600 feet.
Length	3.8 miles one way
Trail Details	Paved road. One option is to ride up on the tram, then walk down. The tram makes nine stops along the route. You can get out at any stop and reboard at any stop.
Features	Excellent stands of huge saguaros, rocky cliffs, and flowing water.

Trail	**BEAR CANYON TRAIL / SABINO DAM TRAIL / SABINO CANYON**
Difficulty	Moderate
Length	Approximately 3 miles
Trail Details	From the Visitor Center take Bear Canyon Trail. This is a wide, sandy, flat trail. (Wheelchairs and strollers can be used on this trail for a short distance.) At the intersection with the paved

Bear Canyon tram road is a trail marker giving distances to Sabino Dam, Bluff Trail, and Creek Trail. Take this route across to Sabino Canyon. Restrooms and picnic benches are along the way. In about a mile you will meet Sabino Canyon tram road. Walk down the road back to the Visitor Center.

Features   The trail takes you through desert vegetation into riparian habitat along the river. Large trees and water attract many species of birds. The unpaved route is less crowded than the roads.

ROY P. DRACHMAN – AGUA CALIENTE PARK

Area	Northeast
Agency/Org	Pima County Parks and Recreation
Fee	None
Address	12325 East Roger Road
Directions	Drive east on Tanque Verde Road. Turn north on Soldier Trail. Turn east on Roger Road to the park entrance which is on the left (north) side of the road.
Facilities	Flush toilets, drinking fountain, picnic benches.

Trail	**LOOP TRAILS**
Difficulty	Easy; paved wheelchair access to pond two
Length	Total length of all trails approximately 1 mile.
Trail Details	Orientation map and bird list available near restrooms.
Features	The park encompasses 101 acres. A natural spring provides a refreshing riparian habitat. Bird viewing opportunities vary with the season. Level trails wind through natural desert permitting access around three ponds. These ponds contain several exotic species of fish and turtles. Portions of the rich habitat are closed to the public to allow corridors for javelina, mule deer, and bobcat that use the park. The ranch house and caretaker cottage will soon be renovated.

SKY CLUB WASH NATURAL AREA

Area	Sunrise Drive near Swan
Agency/Org	Catalina Foothills High School
Fee	None
Address	4300 E Sunrise Drive
Directions	3 blocks west of Swan Blvd on south side of street
Facilities	None

Trail	**SKY CLUB WASH INTERPRETIVE TRAIL**
Difficulty	Easy
Length	Approximately 1 mile
Trail Details	Trail begins immediately west of the parking area. An interpretive sign shows a map of the trail.
Features	The trail was built and is maintained by high school students and is part of the Arizona Trail System. Twelve acres of Sonoran desert scrub and dry wash habitat nestle between the high school and busy Pontatoc Road. Interpretive signs tell of wash conservation and desert life. Plant life is quite varied and includes palo verde, canyon ragweed, desert hackberry, mistletoe, desert broom, Mormon tea, and creosote bush. Birds, lizards, and small mammals find refuge in this preserve.

SOUTHEAST

LINCOLN PARK

Area	Southeast
Agency/Org	Tucson Parks and Recreation Department
Fee	None
Address	8280 East Escalante Road
Directions	Drive south on Pantano Road. Turn left (east) at Escalante. Drive past Santa Rita High School. Look to your right (south). About .7 mile is the entrance to the park. Park in the parking area; trailhead signs are across the playing field.
Facilities	Flush toilets, group picnic area, benches along the trails.

Trails	**HANDICAPPED TRAIL, RIDGE TRAIL, RIPARIAN TRAIL**
Difficulty	Easy; one trail is wheelchair accessible
Length	Each loop trail is approximately .25 mile
Trail Details	A trail map is posted at the trailhead. The Handicapped Trail provides a flat, dirt trail along desert habitat. The Ridge Trail continues from the handicapped trail. A gentle climb provides views of the nearby Rincon Mountains and the Santa Catalinas. The Riparian Trail leads along a wash.
Features	Santa Rita High School and urban neighborhoods and busy streets are nearby, but once inside the park the Atturbury Bird and Animal Sanctuary provide a quiet, pleasant respite. Here native vegetation and animal habitat are preserved. Trails

wind through natural desert. Large mesquites and desert hack-berry line the wash and provide good examples of riparian habitat. Signs along the trails label and interpret plants, packrat nests and squirrel burrows.

SOUTHWEST

JOHN F. KENNEDY REGIONAL PARK

Area	Southwest
Agency/Org	Tucson Parks and Recreation Department
Fee	None
Address	Ajo Way and Mission Road
Directions	The Park is located on the northwest corner of Mission Road and Ajo Way. Access is from Mission Road, or from Cholla Blvd (one block west of Mission Road).
Facilities	Toilets, water fountains, picnic areas are wheelchair accessible.

Trail	**NO OFFICIAL TRAIL**
Difficulty	Easy
Trail Details	In the western side of the park unpaved trails are scattered throughout the picnic area and to the hills beyond the fiesta area west of Cholla Blvd.
Features	There are no interpretive trails, but paths through desert areas allow for closeup views of desert vegetation and signs of animal life. The lake at the east end of the park attracts many species of water birds.

CENTRAL

TUCSON BOTANICAL GARDENS

Area	Central
Agency/Org	Tucson Botanical Gardens
Fee	Entrance fee. Children under five free. Memberships available.
Address	2150 North Alvernon Way
Directions	TBG is on Alvernon south of Grant Road on the east side of the street.
Facilities	Toilets, drinking fountains, benches

Trail	**WALKWAYS THROUGHOUT THE GARDENS**
Difficulty	Easy, wheelchair accessible
Length	Total length of trails approximately 1 mile
Trail Details	Paved, flat walkways
Features	Themed gardens include: herbs, xeriscape plants, flowers that attract birds and butterflies, traditional Tohono O'odham and barrio plantings, a children's garden, and a tropical forest exhibit. The use of desert plantings in garden settings are emphasized. This oasis surrounded by busy, noisy streets illustrates how vegetation can muffle traffic sounds and attract birdlife. A gift shop and plant sale area are on the grounds.

189

Those who dwell among the beauties and mysteries of the Earth are never alone or weary of life.

—Rachael Carson

Phoenix

Compiled and written by

Thomas Hulen Desert Botanical Garden, Phoenix

WEST

White Tank Regional Park
- Goat Canyon
- Waterfall
- Black Rock

EAST

Usery Mountain Recreation Area
- Merkle
- Wind Cave

Superstition Wilderness
- Peralta
- Garden Valley

Lost Dutchman State Park
- Treasure Loop

Squaw Peak Park
- Squaw Peak Nature Trail
- Squaw Peak
- Dreamy Draw Nature Trail

NORTH

Echo Canyon Recreation Area
(Camelback Mountain)
- Echo Canyon Trail
- Camelback Mountain Trail

SOUTH

South Mountain Park and Preserve
- Holbert Trail
- Kiwanis Trail
- Buena Vista to Natural Tunnel
- Mormon Trail
- Pima Canyon
- Pima Canyon to Natural Tunnel
- Telegraph Pass

CENTRAL

Desert Botanical Garden
- The Desert Discovery Trail
- Plants and People of the Sonoran Desert
- Sonoran Desert Nature Trail

The Phoenix Zoo

Pueblo Grande Museum and Cultural Park

WEST

WHITE TANK MOUNTAINS

Area	White Tank Regional Park
Agency/Org	Maricopa County Parks and Recreation Department
Fee	Yes
Restrictions	Dogs must be on a leash, no glass containers.
Directions	The park is located 15 miles west of Peoria, Arizona on Olive Avenue. It may be reached from I-10 by taking Cotton Lane north 7 miles to Olive Avenue and then west 5 miles to park entrance. Pick up a park map at the entrance, or look at the map on display.
Facilities	Restrooms, picnic and camping areas, and drinking fountains.
Note	There are over 20 miles of maintained trails in the White Tank Mountain Regional Park. All trails are variable in length and difficulty and most are open for equestrian and bicycle use. This park features some of the most beautiful and intact Sonoran Desert in the Phoenix area. A sizeable herd of desert mule deer lives within the park. Park visitors frequently see deer and their sign along the trails and near springs.

Trail	**GOAT CANYON**
Directions	The Goat Canyon trailhead can be accessed from Picnic Areas 1 and 7, forming a partial loop trail.
Difficulty	Most of this trail is moderate in difficulty. From Picnic Area 1 the trail is fairly flat and easy for about 1 mile.
Length	6.5 miles from Picnic Areas 1 and 7 roundtrip
Trail Details	This trail is rocky and steep in most places. Most hikers use the trailhead at picnic area 1 and return to it after reaching the rock corrals.
Features	Spectacular examples of upper Sonoran desert vegetation and wildlife can be seen from this trail. Near the halfway point on this trail are some examples of rock corrals used by goat herders during the early part of the 20th century.

Trail	**WATERFALL**
Directions	The trailhead is accessed from Picnic Area 6.
Difficulty	Most of this trail is quite easy. The last 50 yards involves climbing a few steps. The first half of the trail is wheelchair accessible.

Length	2 mile roundtrip
Trail Details	The first half of this trail has a hardened surface and several benches.
Features	The White Tank Mountains gets it name from the tinaja or tank at the end of this trail. Used by several generations of people as a reliable source of water, this ancient trail, lined by the petroglyphs of the archaic, Patayan, and Hohokam people, winds through a desert canyon to the tank. Falling over 30 feet into the tank is a waterfall that offers visitors a spectacular sight during rainy periods. Most years a number of aquatic insects and plants can be reliably found here because the tank contains water year round.

Trail	**BLACK ROCK**
Directions	Trailhead starts at Picnic Area 4.
Difficulty	The short loop of this trail is wheelchair accessible and easy.
Length	.5 mile
Trail Details	The short loop has a hardened surface.
Features	This trail features interpretive signs relating information about the local flora and ancient petroglyphs.

EAST

USERY MOUNTAINS

Area	Usery Mountain Recreation Area
Agency/Org	Maricopa County Parks and Recreation Department
Fee	Yes
Restrictions	Dogs must be on a leash, no glass containers
Directions	This park is located northeast of Mesa, Arizona. Take U.S. 60 (Superstition Freeway) to Ellsworth Road. Travel north to Usery Pass Road and the park entrance. Be sure to pick up a map at the entrance.
Facilities	Restrooms, picnic and camping facilities, drinking fountains.
Note	There are nearly 30 miles of trails in this area. All trails are variable in length and difficulty. Horseback riding is allowed on most trails.

Trail	MERKLE
Directions	The trailhead is at picnic area 6.
Difficulty	Easy to moderate, some slight grade changes through desert washes.

Length	1 mile loop
Features	This short hike has signs that interpret the local flora. This trail passes through a desert wash. Washes are great places to see animal sign such as tracks and feces because animals use these areas as thoroughfares. Check out the banks for sign of burrowing by mammals and insects.

Trail	**WIND CAVE**
Directions	The trailhead is on the north end of Wind Cave Drive. The trail can also be accessed from the Group Picnic Area.
Difficulty	Moderate
Length	3.5 mile roundtrip
Trail Details	This trail has an elevation gain of about 800 feet. Plants and animals commonly associated with desert bajadas are found here. Wind Cave is not a true cave, but rather a rock shelter carved out of the mountain by the action of the wind and rain.

SUPERSTITION MOUNTAINS

Area	Superstition Wilderness
Agency/Org	Tonto National Forest, United States Department of Agriculture
Fee	Yes
Restrictions	Dogs must be on a leash.

Trail	**PERALTA**
Directions	Take U.S. 60 east of Apache Junction to Peralta Road. Turn north and travel approximately 7 miles to the Peralta Trail trailhead.
Difficulty	Moderate
Length	4.5 miles roundtrip to Fremont Saddle
Trail Details	The trail is steep in some areas and should be avoided when wet, particularly during the rainy seasons. This trail intersects a desert wash, which floods periodically.
Features	This is one of the most popular trails in central Arizona and therefore can be quite crowded on the weekends during the spring and fall. Hikers experience three plant communities while hiking this trail. The lower part of the trail is dominated by typical upper Sonoran Desert vegetation such as palo verde, cat claw acacia and numerous species of cacti. Portions that intersect the wash will have riparian plants such as

194

netleaf hackberry, willow, cottonwood and seep willow. At Fremont Saddle chaparral plants, such as buck brush, manzanita, shrub oak, pinyon pine and juniper trees can be found. The view is fantastic from Fremont Saddle. To the northwest is the eroded volcano core known as Weaver's Needle. Hikers can continue on from here or return to the trailhead.

The Superstition Mountains contain hundreds of miles of trails. Most of them are in good condition, but require that hikers be in good physical shape and well prepared. Outdoor specialty stores and bookstores offer a number of books and maps that focus on the Superstition Mountains. It is strongly recommended that hikers familiarize themselves with this information before exploring deeply in this mountain range.

Trail	**GARDEN VALLEY**
Directions	From U.S. 60 take the Idaho Road exit and travel north to the famed Apache Trail (Arizona 88); turn right and drive to the First Water turnoff. Drive about 3 miles to the First Water Trailhead. Take the Second Water Trail.
Facilities	None
Difficulty	Easy to moderate
Length	4 miles
Trail Details	This trail is fairly steep in some areas, but if taken slowly to enjoy the wonderful landscape, hikers with modest ability will find this trail most interesting and worthwhile. The trail is rocky and can be slick when wet.
Features	This trail is a must for people interested in seeing the spring flower display. After hiking 2 miles hikers encounter Garden Valley. This area has been used by countless generations as a farm and village site. Look carefully for pottery sherds along the trail, but please remember that collecting of prehistoric artifacts is illegal on public land. Besides if you leave artifacts where they lay other lucky hikers will have a chance to see and appreciate a bit of prehistory.

Hikers seeking additional adventure can continue on other trails from this area.

SUPERSTITION MOUNTAINS

Area	Lost Dutchman State Park
Agency/Org	Arizona State Parks
Fee	Yes
Restrictions	Dogs must be on a leash.
Directions	From U.S. 60 take the Idaho Road exit in Apache Junction. Travel north to the Apache Trail (Arizona 88) and turn right. The entrance to the park is a few miles to the east.
Facilities	Restrooms, picnic and camping area and drinking fountains
Note	There are several good trails in this park; all are connected. The trails provide the hiker with a very nice opportunity to experience the Sonoran Desert. It is highly recommended that park visitors pick up a trail map at the entrance. Those interested in a more challenging hike should take the Siphon Draw Trail. See the park map for details.

This is one of the best places to experience springtime desert wildflower displays. |

Trail	**TREASURE LOOP**
Directions	The trailhead is located at the Cholla Day Use Area.
Difficulty	Easy
Trail Details	Parts of the trail are rocky. There is about a 500-foot elevation gain.
Length	2.4 mile loop
Features	Hikers witness the beauty of a typical Sonoran Desert bajada on this trail. Cacti of many species are seen, particularly the noble saguaro and dense stands of chain-fruit cholla. Near the halfway point the rocks are covered with lichen and algae.

Site	**SQUAW PEAK**
Area	Squaw Peak Park
Agency/Org	City of Phoenix Parks, Recreation and Library Department
Fee	No
Restrictions	Pets must be on a leash, no glass containers.
Directions	From the Squaw Peak Parkway (Arizona 51), take the Lincoln Drive exit and travel east to Squaw Peak Drive. Turn left and travel north to the park entrance and continue to the Apache Ramada. The trailhead is located nearby.
Facilities	Restrooms, picnic areas and drinking fountains.

Trail	**SQUAW PEAK NATURE TRAIL**

Difficulty   Easy

Length   1.5 miles loop

Trail Details   There is a nearly 200-foot elevation gain on this trail.

Features   This is a great trail for people who want a quick hike into the Sonoran Desert. It is hard to believe that Squaw Peak is surrounded by nearly two million people when hiking this trail. Plants typical of the Sonoran desert are encountered; the washes are good places to spot wildlife. Some of the plants are identified with signs. The ancient Hohokam people who once lived in the Phoenix area traveled to this area to collect schist — the rock that breaks off in thin sheets — for stone tools. Remember, if you encounter any artifacts please do take them with you; leave them for some other person to ponder over and appreciate.

SQUAW PEAK

Area   Dreamy Draw Park

Agency   City of Phoenix Parks, Recreation and Library Department

Fee   No

Restrictions   Pets must be on a leash. No glass containers.

Directions   From the Squaw Peak Freeway (Arizona 51), take the Northern Avenue exit east to the Dreamy Draw Park. The trailhead is on the north side of the parking lot.

Facilities   Restrooms, picnic area, and drinking fountain.

Trail   **DREAMY DRAW NATURE TRAIL**

Difficulty   Easy

Length   1.5 miles

Features   This is easy trail for hikers who want quick access to the Sonoran Desert. Note the schist rock that breaks off in thin sheets. Ancient Hohokam craftspeople used this material for making tools. The trail wanders through a desert wash that is dominated by mesquite, palo verde, and ironwood trees. When it rains much of the water that strikes the mountain's surface area eventually ends up in a wash like this one, thus enabling these trees to thrive in this area. As in all washes, note the banks. Solitary bees and wasps can be seen excavating nests in these areas.

NORTH

ECHO CANYON RECREATION AREA

Area	Camelback Mountain
Agency/Org	City of Phoenix Parks, Recreation and Library Department
Fee	None
Restrictions	Dogs must be on a leash. No glass containers.
Directions	From I-10 take Arizona 143 north to 44th Street exit. Travel north about seven miles until 44th Street turns into Tatum Boulevard. The entrance is just east of MacDonald Drive on Tatum Boulevard.
Facilities	Interpretive ramada and drinking fountain. There are no restrooms or picnic facilities.
Note	There are three public trails at Camelback Mountain. All are considered difficult and are for experienced hikers.

Trail	**ECHO CANYON TRAIL**
Difficulty	Difficult, not wheelchair accessible
Length	.12 mile
Trail Details	This trail is short and quite steep in places. It is not paved.
Features	Echo Canyon is a natural rock shelter that resembles a band shell carved into the side of a mountain. Many older maps refer to the canyon as a ceremonial grotto because local Indians used it for ritual presentations. Many species of plants no longer found naturally in the rest of the Phoenix area can be found along this trail.

Trail	**CAMELBACK MOUNTAIN TRAIL**
Difficulty	Difficult, very steep and not wheelchair accessible. Elevation varies from 1,440 feet at the trailhead to 2,704 feet at the summit of Camelback Mountain.
Trail Length	1.16 miles
Trail Details	It is not paved and is very steep.
Features	On clear days this trail offers some spectacular vistas of the Phoenix area. Prairie Falcons are frequently spotted on this trail. Whitewash can be seen on the cliffs above their nests.

SOUTH

SOUTH MOUNTAIN

Area	South Mountain Park/Preserve
Agency/Org	City of Phoenix Parks, Recreation and Library Department
Fee	None
Restrictions	Pets must be on a leash. No glass containers.
Directions	From I-10 take the Central Avenue exit and drive south on Central Avenue to the Park entrance where Central Avenue ends.
Facilities	Restrooms, picnic areas, drinking fountains and interpretive center.
Note	There are over 50 miles of trails in South Mountain Park; they vary greatly in length and difficulty. Horse rental is available, and many trails are open to mountain bikes. All of the trails offer spectacular Sonoran Desert landscape with many trails passing by abandoned mines, some of which are fairly deep. (Under no circumstances should hikers explore these mines.) Javelinas are common near springs, picnic areas, and irrigated landscapes.

Trail	**HOLBERT TRAIL**
Directions	Enter the Park on Central Avenue, turn left just past the gate house and park on the east end of the Activity Center parking lot near the restrooms. The trailhead is south of this area and is marked by a sign.
Difficulty	The first half of the trail is easy and fairly flat. Most of this part is wheelchair accessible. The second half is steep, gains about 1,000 feet in elevation, and is not wheelchair accessible.
Length	Approximately 5 miles roundtrip
Trail Details	This trail is not paved and can be muddy during wet conditions.
Features	The first half of this trail features some spectacular Hohokam petroglyphs; most can be seen easily from the trail. Binoculars are helpful to see the petroglyphs located high on the canyon walls. Various plants common to the Sonoran Desert line the second half of the trail. Rock squirrels, Harris' antelope squirrels and packrat middens are frequent sights along this segment. A stone building constructed by the Civilian Conservation Corps in the late 1930s marks Dobbin's Lookout, the end of the trail. The Salt River Valley can be seen from the lookout on clear days.

Trail	**KIWANIS TRAIL**
Directions	On Central Avenue stop at the gatehouse at the Park's entrance and ask for a trail map, or pass the gatehouse and turn left at the third road, about 1 mile, and head south to the trailhead, which is marked by a sign.
Difficulty	Moderate and not wheelchair accessible.
Length	2 miles
Trail Details	This unpaved trail is steep and rocky in places. People with moderate physical ability can easy hike this trail if they take it slowly.
Features	This was originally a trail used by local Indians to pass through the mountains on their trips to and from the Salt and Gila River basins. A number of petroglyphs are encountered along the way. In the late 1930s the Civilian Conservation Corps built a number of flood control dams along the trail; these are currently filled with sediment. This is an excellent place to see the erosional effects of water in desert mountains. At the top of the trail is an area known as Telegraph Pass. This is the site where the first telegraph line connecting Phoenix with communities to the south was located. Hikers can descend down the 1.5 mile Telegraph Pass Trail at this point, or return the way they came.

Trail	**BUENA VISTA TO NATURAL TUNNEL**
Directions	Enter the Park on Central Avenue and continue up to the top of South Maintain via the Summit Road. Follow this road eastward until it ends at a small parking lot and a trailhead marker.
Facilities	None
Difficulty	Moderate and not wheelchair accessible.
Length	3.5 miles roundtrip
Trail Details	This trail is steep in some places. Watch out for mountain bikes.
Features	The highlight of this trail is a natural tunnel carved out of granite by water. There are many other examples in Hidden Valley of how water can sculpture the landscape in this normally dry area. Encountered along the trail and marked by a sign is an area known as Fat Man Pass. The pass and tunnel are great destinations for a picnic.

Trail	MORMON TRAIL
Directions	From I-10 take the 24th Street exit and follow 24th Street until it ends at South Mountain Park. The trailhead is located at the south end of 24th Street.
Facilities	None
Difficulty	Moderate and not wheelchair accessible.
Length	2.2 miles roundtrip
Trail Details	This trail is steep and rocky and should be avoided when wet.
Features	This trail offers a quick and easy way to see a Sonoran Desert bajada environment. Vegetation differences between bajadas and desert canyons are quite obvious on this trail. Packrat nests and ringtail cats are frequently seen on this trail. Keep an eye out for petroglyphs; they are not along the trail, but can been seen on nearby rock outcrops.

Trail	PIMA CANYON
Directions	From I-10 take the Baseline Road exit and drive east to 56th Street, also called Avenida del Yaqui. Drive south on 56th Street through the Yaqui village of Guadalupe to Guadalupe Road. Turn right and drive for about 1 mile to 48th Street. The entrance to Pima Canyon is about 100 feet north of Guadalupe Road on 48th Street on the extreme east end of the South Mountain range.
Facilities	Ramadas, picnic tables, drinking fountains, and restrooms.
Note	Pima Canyon is the trailhead for several trails on the east side of South Mountain Park. Located near the trailhead and marked by a sign is the famous Marcos de Niza Inscription Rock. Today most scholars believe the inscriptions are not authentic; many in the local Hispanic community, however, look to the site as a monument to the Spanish contribution to the Southwest.

Trail	PIMA CANYON TO NATURAL TUNNEL
Directions	From the Pima Canyon Trailhead travel west on dirt road, 1.2 miles, to National Trail Trailhead. (Only maintenance and emergency vehicles are allowed on this road which travels the length of Pima Canyon.) Near the end of this road is a wildlife watering station that was established for the javelina living in this area. At the National Trail Trailhead continue westward for about 2 miles. Turn left at the Hidden Valley Trail for a short distance. See Buena Vista to Natural Tunnel trail for details.

Difficulty	The first 1.2 miles on the dirt road is easy and wheelchair accessible. The National Trail at that point is moderate in difficulty and quite steep in some places.
Length	5.5 miles roundtrip
Trail Details	This is a favorite trail for mountain bike enthusiasts. Hikers must therefore remain watchful while traveling here.
Features	There are a number of Hohokam petroglyphs found along the edges of Pima Canyon; binoculars are helpful in locating them. Many hikers prefer to hike up the bottom of Pima Canyon; it is slightly more difficult to hike but it provides a better opportunity to see plant and animal life common to desert washes. The sandy wash is not wheelchair accessible. The road is a good place to compare the difference between north- and south-facing slopes. Notice how much more dense and woody the vegetation is on the north-facing slope compared to the south-facing side. Rock squirrels are frequently encountered on this trail. Listen for their chatter as they perch on nearby boulders.

Trail	**TELEGRAPH PASS**
Directions	The trailhead is located on the south side of South Mountain. From I-10 take Chandler Boulevard west to Desert Foothills Parkway. Follow this road north about 2 miles. The City of Phoenix Parks, Recreation and Library Department maintains a parking lot near the end of Desert Foothills Parkway.
Facilities	Drinking fountain
Difficulty	Easy, wheelchair accessible, but steep in one area.
Trail Details	Approximately .5 mile of this trail is paved.
Length	3 miles roundtrip
Features	Climbing to the top of Telegraph Pass this trail passes by Hohokam petroglyphs. One petroglyph features a large image of a bighorn sheep. Bighorn sheep inhabited this range well into historic times; former lambing sites are located nearby. This trail offers hikers a chance to see an elephant tree, Bursera microphylla. At one time it was thought that South Mountain's elephant trees were the most northerly population recorded. Today they are found further north, but the elephant trees along this trail are the easiest for hikers to see.

Hikers interested in the differences in vegetation of north versus south-facing slopes should hike up to Telegraph Pass and compare the differences in kinds and quantities of cacti found on each slope. The south side of the mountain has many more kinds and a greater numbers of cacti. The northern slope has very few cold intolerant elephant trees. The trail on the north side is the Kiwanis Trail.

CENTRAL

DESERT BOTANICAL GARDEN

Area	Papago Park, Phoenix, Arizona
Agency/Org	Desert Botanical Garden (private, nonprofit)
Fee	Entrance fee, children under five are free, memberships are available.
Restrictions	No pets or food.
Directions	From Arizona 202 (Red Mountain Freeway), take the Priest Road exit and travel north to Galvin Parkway. Priest turns into Galvin Parkway at Washington Street. The address is 1201 North Galvin Parkway, Phoenix, AZ 85008
Facilities	Restrooms, drinking fountains, restaurant, and gift shop are available. Picnic facilities are not available on site, but an excellent picnic area is nearby. Ask the admissions staff for directions.
Note	There is slightly more than 1 mile of trail at the Desert Botanical Garden. Each trail has several unique features that illustrate the natural history of the Sonoran Desert. The Garden has over 20,000 desert plants on display. Wildlife is abundant: the Garden is a hotspot for local birders with 114 species recorded. In addition, 16 species of reptiles, 3 species of amphibians and 12 species of mammals have been seen here.

Trail	**THE DESERT DISCOVERY TRAIL**
Difficulty	Easy, wheelchair accessible
Length	.33 mile loop
Trail Details	Brick-paved with slight grade changes.
Features	This is the Garden's main trail; all other trails and facilities are linked by this trail. On this trail visitors will find desert plants from around the world.
	Interpretive displays are available that explain desert formation and how plants adapt to arid conditions.

Trail	**PLANTS AND PEOPLE OF THE SONORAN DESERT**
Difficulty	Easy, wheelchair accessible
Length	.25 mile loop
Trail Details	Paved with stabilized decomposed granite, mostly level.
Features	The trail is dedicated to Native American use of Sonoran Desert plants. An O'odham round house and two Apache wickiups constructed of native materials are highlights of this trail.

Trail	**SONORAN DESERT NATURE TRAIL**
Difficulty	Easy, wheelchair accessible
Length	.33 mile loop
Trail Details	Paved and steep
Features	The trail is a great introduction to the Sonoran Desert. It focuses on the plants and animals of this region with engaging exhibits, dramatic vistas, and close-up examination of the plants and animals common in this area.

THE PHOENIX ZOO

Area	Papago Park
Agency/Org	The Phoenix Zoo (private, nonprofit)
Fee	Yes
Directions	From Arizona 202 take the Priest Road exit and travel north. Priest turns into Galvin Parkway at Washington Street. The address is 455 North Galvin Parkway.
Restrictions	No pets or outside food.
Facilities	Restrooms, restaurant, drinking fountains.

Trails	**ARIZONA TRAIL AND DESERT LIVE**
Difficulty	Easy and wheelchair accessible.
Length	1 mile
Features	Individuals and families interested in Sonoran Desert wildlife should consider a visit to the Phoenix Zoo. There are many examples of desert animals in the many life-like exhibits. While most of the animals displayed are common to this region, most area residents will not have the opportunity to see them in the wild.

PUEBLO GRANDE MUSEUM AND CULTURAL PARK

Area	Pueblo Grande Museum and Cultural Park
Agency/Org	City of Phoenix Parks, Recreation and Library Department
Fee	Yes
Restrictions	No pets or glass containers.
Directions	From Arizona 143 take the Washington Street exit and go west. The address is 4619 E. Washington Street.

Trail	**OUTDOOR**
Difficulty	Easy and wheelchair accessible.
Length	.66 mile
Trail details	Paved with slight grade variations.
Features	This is a great trail for those who want to learn more about the ancient Hohokam people who lived in this area from around A.D.1 to 1450. Actual ruins can be seen as well as an authentic full-scale exhibit featuring Hohokam building styles. The museum has several exhibits that interpret Hohokam culture.

We shall not cease from exploration
and the end of all our exploring
will be to arrive where we started…
and know the place for the first time.

— T. S. Eliot

Additional Information

Take nothing but pictures.
Leave nothing but footprints.
Kill nothing but time.

— Motto of the Baltimore Grotto,
a caving society

FAMILY ACTIVITIES ON THE TRAIL AND AT HOME

There are many adventures along the trail — new sights, sounds, and smells, and so much to discover. Because simple sensory activities enhance the experience, we have included a number of them on our website, **www.desertmuseum.org**. Log on, go to publications, and take a look.

One of the activities your family can do while on the trail is "Tuning In." It helps develop awareness of nature. Another activity you'll find on our website is "The Amazing Expanding Saguaros." This hands-on exercise shows you what rain in the desert does to saguaros. It really is amazing!

During your outings you studied nature firsthand and learned about the plants and animals that inhabit the desert. You shared adventures with your family, enjoyed a snack along the trail, and maybe took some photos. How can you save the memories of these special days? One means is by assembling an album of snapshots, notations, and poems. See "A Family Adventure Album" and "Desert Poetry" for ideas. Projects that develop creativity and research skills are also included on the Desert Museum website.

Share the activities with the whole family. Get everybody involved! The results may very well become treasured mementos of your desert adventures.

Saguaro so tall / arms reaching to the sky. / If only you could / see and speak — what stories / you could tell me / as you watch the / desert world / pass by / your rooted feet.

Poetry Patterns

Finger Critters

Suncatchers

209

SUGGESTED READING

Many good books about the Sonoran Desert are in print with new ones being published all the time. It is impractical to include a complete list here, so we suggest you browse through your school and neighborhood libraries or favorite bookstores or visit our website (www.desertmuseum.org) for a more complete bibliography.

Here is a brief list of suggested titles that will help you and your children interpret the fascinating world along desert trails.

Field Guides

Here are some of the popular field guide series:

- Golden Guides (New York: Golden Books Publishing Company)
- Easy Field Guides (Phoenix: Primer Publishers)
- National Audubon Society Field Guides (New York: Alfred A. Knopf)
- Peterson Field Guides (Boston: Houghton Mifflin)

There are also a number of field guides aimed at children. Two popular series:

- National Audubon First Field Guides (New York: Scholastic)
- Peterson Field Guides for Young Naturalists (Boston: Houghton Mifflin)

Two other fun Sonoran Desert field guides:

Merlin, Pinau
1999 *A Field Guide to Desert Holes*. Tucson: Arizona-Sonora Desert Museum Press.

Merlin, Pinau
2001 *A Guide to Southern Arizona Bird Nests & Eggs*. Tucson: Arizona-Sonora Desert Museum Press.

Informative Books for Adults and Older Children

Arizona-Sonora Desert Museum
2000 *A Natural History of the Sonoran Desert.* Tucson: Arizona-Sonora Desert Museum Press. Co-published with The University of California Press. (*This is the most complete collection of Sonoran Desert natural history information currently available.*)

Evans, Doris and Jesus García
1998 *Desert Life, A Vocabulary/Vida Desertica, Vocabulario.* Tucson: Arizona-Sonora Desert Museum Press. (*English-Spanish and Spanish-English translations for hundreds of natural history words with the emphasis on Sonoran Desert terms.*)

Hanson, Jonathan and
Roseann Beggy Hanson
1996 *Southern Arizona Nature Almanac.* Boulder, CO: Pruett Publishing Company. (*A seasonal guide to Pima County and beyond. Each chapter covers a month's worth of natural happenings you are likely to experience.*)

Lazaroff, David Wentworth
1998 *Arizona-Sonora Desert Museum Book of Answers.* Tucson: Arizona-Sonora Desert Museum Press. (*Detailed answers to questions that the staff at the Desert Museum most often hear.*)

Olin, George
1994 *House in the Sun: A Natural History of the Sonoran Desert.* Tucson: Southwest Parks and Monuments Association. (*The Sonoran Desert is the "house in the sun." Longtime naturalist George Olin explores the many facets of its ecological story.*)

Werner, Floyd and Carl Olson
1994 *Learning About Living with Insects of the Southwest.* Tucson: Fisher Books. (*Describes and illustrates over 120 of the most common arthropods likely to share your home and neighborhood.*)

Books for Young Children

There are scores of children's books about the desert. These are a few of our favorites.

Bash, Barbara
1990 *Desert Giant: The World of the Saguaro Cactus.*
Boston: Little, Brown and Company.

Marsh, T.J. and Jennifer Ward
1998 Way Out in the Desert. Flagstaff: Rising Moon.
(This is the Sonoran Desert version of "Over in the Meadow...")

Moreillon, Judy
1997 *Sing Down the Rain.* Santa Fe: Kiva Publishing Company.
(Written as a poem with illustrations by Tohono O'odham artist, Michael Chiago, tell of the annual summer ceremony. Wine is made from saguaro fruit and all dance in a circle to ask for plentiful rain.)

National Geographic Society
1995 *Creatures of the Desert World.*
Washington D.C.: National Geographic Society.
(Pop-up book full of Sonoran Desert plants and animals.)

Zoehfeld, Kathleen Weidner
1997 *Cactus Cafe.* Norwalk, CT: Trudy Corporation.
(The saguaro cactus as an important food and nesting site for many desert animals.)

Activities

Olmstead, Adrienne
2000 *My Nature Journal: A Personal Nature Guide for Young People.*
Lafayette, CA: Pajaro.
(Children can write and sketch in this easy-to-carry journal. Ideas for journal entries are attractively presented throughout the book. Spiral binding makes it easy to use.)

TUCSON AREA AGENCIES AND ORGANIZATIONS

These Tucson area organizations offer information on trails and natural history programs.

Arizona-Sonora Desert Museum
2021 West Kinney Road
Tucson, AZ 85743-8918
(520) 883-1380
Website: www.desertmuseum.org

Catalina State Park
11570 North Oracle Road
Tucson, AZ 85737
(520) 628-5798

Coronado National Forest
Forest Service Office
300 West Congress
Tucson, AZ 85701
(520) 670-4552

Coronado National Forest
Sabino Canyon
5700 North Santa Catalina Road
Tucson, AZ 85715
(520) 749-8700

Pima County Parks and Recreation Department
1204 West Silverlake Road
Tucson, AZ 85713
(520) 740-2690

Saguaro National Park
East District Visitors Center
3693 Old Spanish Trail Road
Tucson, AZ 85730-5601
(520) 733-5153
Website: www.nps.gov/sagu
Website for Friends of Saguaro National Park: www.azstarnet.com/~fosnp

Saguaro National Park
West District Visitors Center
2700 North Kinney Road
Tucson, AZ 85743
(520) 733-5158

Tohono Chul
7366 North Paseo del Norte
Tucson, AZ 85704-4415
(520) 575-8468
Website: www.tohonochulpark.org

Tucson Audubon Society
300 East University Blvd. #120
Tucson, AZ 85705
(520) 629-0510
Website: www.audubon.org/chapter/az/tucson
Website for Mason Audubon Center: www.azstarnet.com/~audubon/mason-center

Tucson Botanical Gardens
2150 North Alvernon Way
Tucson, AZ 85712
(520) 326-9255
Website: www.tucson botanical.org

Tucson, City of
Parks and Recreation
900 South Randolph Way
Tucson, AZ 85716
(520) 791-4873
Website: ci.tucson.az.us/parksandrec/

PHOENIX AREA AGENCIES AND ORGANIZATIONS

These Phoenix area organizations offer information on trails and natural history programs.

Arizona State Parks
1300 West Washington
Phoenix, AZ 85007
(602) 542-4174
Website: www.pr.state.az.us

City of Phoenix Parks, Recreation, and Library Department
Phoenix City Hall
200 West Washington Street, 16th Floor
Phoenix, AZ 85003
(602) 262-6862
Website:
www.ci.phoenix.az.us/PARKS/offices

Desert Botanical Gardens
1201 North Galvin Parkway
Phoenix, AZ 85008
(480) 941-1225
Website: www.dbg.org

Echo Canyon Recreation Area
East McDonald Drive at Tatum Blvd.
Phoenix, AZ
(602) 256-3110
Website: See City of Phoenix Parks

Lost Dutchman State Park
(480) 982-4485
Website: See Arizona State Parks

Maricopa County Parks and Recreation Department
3475 West Durango Street
Phoenix, AZ 85009
(602) 506-2930
Website: www.maricopa.gov/rec

The Phoenix Zoo
455 Galvin North Parkway
Phoenix, AZ 85008
(602) 273-1341
Website: phoenixzoo.com

South Mountain Park
10919 South Central Avenue
Phoenix, AZ 85040
Website: See City of Phoenix Parks

Tonto National Forest
2324 East McDowell Road
Phoenix, AZ 85545
(602) 225-5200
Website: www.fs.fed.us/r3/tonto

Usery Mountain Recreation Area
3939 North Usery
Mesa, AZ 85207
(480) 984-0032
Website: See Maricopa County Parks

White Tank Mountain Regional Park
West Olive Avenue
Wadell, AZ 85355
(623) 935-2505
Website: See Maricopa County Parks

LEARNING TO USE BINOCULARS

Binoculars are precision instruments; children will value and treasure them if they learn how to care for and use them properly.

Care of binoculars:
- Do not touch the lenses with fingers or any objects.
- Do not clean lenses with any material other than lens-cleaning fluid and lens-cleaning tissue.
- Keep the strap around your neck at all times.
- Do not bump the binoculars against anything or drop them.

Adjusting binoculars:
- Set the diopter (rotating lens) so that the dot and 0 line up.
- Move the hinged sides until your eyes feel comfortable looking through both lenses.
- Look at a distant object through the binoculars.
- Close the right eye (or cover the right eye piece) and focus the left eye piece by turning the center focus wheel until the view is clear.
- Close the left eye (or cover the left eye piece) and focus the right eye lens with the diopter.
- Now all you have to do is focus with the center wheel.

Viewing objects through the binoculars:
- Look at a distant object with your eyes (the top of a saguaro works well).
- Do not take your eyes from the object as you lift the binoculars to your eyes.

Now that you see clearly with your binoculars you can study birds or other animals. The best way to observe them without scaring them off is to stay still, or move slowly and whisper the location of the animal to the others. Binoculars are wonderful tools for observing the moon, planets, and stars, too.

PHOTO TIPS

Taking the Best Pictures with Your Camera

Photographs are precious souvenirs. They are lasting records of special moments with friends and places we have been. To take good, clear, and pleasing photos, follow these helpful tips.

Many people use the popular "disposable" (one-time-use cameras) or simple "point and shoot" cameras; tips for using these cameras are included here. Avoid the kids' cameras featuring cartoon characters or latest fads; they tend to be inferior quality and frustrating to use. A basic camera for adults works best for children, too. If a camera that requires focusing and light metering, instruct the child in the workings of the camera beforehand.

Distance from Subject

The camera should be no closer than four feet from the subject. Any closer and the picture will be out of focus. The object may look clear in the viewfinder, but most point and shoot cameras cannot focus on something closer than four feet.

Using a Flash

If your camera has a flash, check to see if it automatically flashes or if you must flip a lever to cause the flash to go off.

The flash will work best at distances no closer than six feet from the subject and no farther than about 12 feet. Any closer will make the photo too bright or "washed out." Any farther than 12 feet will give you a photo that is too dark. We can see objects in dim light because our pupils open up to let in more light. Our little cameras have a fixed opening and cannot "see" as well in the dark as we can.

Hold the Camera Steady

Stop, aim, hold the camera firmly, and hold your breath. Then press the shutter. If you keep the camera steady you will have a clear photo. Any movement of the camera as you take your picture will result in a blurry picture.

Frame Your Picture

Think about the picture you see in the viewfinder. Look at your subject. Let's say you are taking a picture of your friend. Be sure you haven't cut off your friend's head. If you want your friend in the center of the photo be sure that's were he or she appears in the viewfinder. If you want your photo to show your friend standing next to a tall saguaro, stand back far enough to include the saguaro from top to bottom. Hold the camera level with the world, otherwise it will look as if your friend and the saguaro are leaning over.

Backgrounds Are Important, Too
Don't forget to look at the background. If you see telephone poles or other unattractive clutter, move the camera to a different angle or move your subject so that you have a pleasant background. If you can see the horizon (where the sky and land meet) in your viewfinder, hold the camera level so the horizon line is straight across the picture.

Is Your Subject Small or Far Away?
You see a rabbit running through the bushes, a bird on a branch, or a hawk circling in the sky and you grab your camera. But, will pictures of these subjects turn out well? The answer is NO. A small, hopping rabbit or a small or faraway bird will be a tiny dot on your photograph. When your pictures are developed you will look at the photo and wonder what it was supposed to be. Those wonderful animal pictures you see in magazines were taken by professional photographers with expensive cameras and lenses.

Don't Cover the Camera Lens
Always be aware of the camera lens as you take your pictures. Be sure nothing is covering the lens such as your finger or piece of your clothing. Everything may look clear through the viewfinder, but the lens is a short distance away. A good rule is to keep your hands on the sides of the camera; then you won't accidently cover the lens with a finger. This rule holds true for the flash, too. A finger covering the flash will give you a very dark photo.

Pace the Snapping
In your excitement to get photos of a special trip it's tempting to take lots of photos right away. But don't use up all of your film the first few minutes of a trip. Pace your snapping. Save film for the middle and the end of the trip as well.

Note on One-Time-Use or Disposable Cameras

These inexpensive little cameras do a remarkably good job for simple point-and-shoot photo taking. Though they're often called disposable, they are not thrown away. They are recycled by the photo companies.

Do not take the film out of the camera. In fact, never open up any part of the camera or you will ruin your film. Take the camera to the photo shop. They will remove the film from the camera and develop it.

If you are taking all of your photos outdoors in sunlight, you do not need to buy a camera with a flash.

If you use 10 or more "disposable" cameras per year, it would be less expensive to buy a small non-disposable camera. There are many good, cheap, easy-to-use cameras available.

NATURE WALK CHECKLIST

Food (packed in zip locked bags)
- [ ] trail mix (gorp) made of a mixture of your favorite cereals, nuts, dried fruits
- [ ] cheese
- [ ] crackers
- [ ] peanut butter sandwich
- [ ] fruit (apple, banana, grapes, orange)
- [ ] carrot, celery sticks
- [ ] prepared trail snacks sweetened with honey or fruits
- [ ] cookies

Liquids (carried in plastic containers)
- [ ] water
  (a quart or liter for every two miles)
- [ ] sport drink or fruit juice

Clothing
- [ ] long pants, long sleeved shirt
- [ ] hat with brim
- [ ] sunglasses
- [ ] bandanna
- [ ] sturdy, comfortable shoes, laces tied
- [ ] thick socks with no holes

First Aid
- [ ] comb for removing a cholla stem
- [ ] tweezers for removing spines
- [ ] bandages
- [ ] first aid cream
- [ ] sunscreen and lip balm (SPF of 15 or more)

Other
- [ ] trash bag
- [ ] camera and enough film
- [ ] binoculars
- [ ] magnifying glass
- [ ] mirror
- [ ] toilet tissue
- [ ] trail map
- [ ] compass
- [ ] notebook and pencils
- [ ] field guides for birds, plants, mammals, reptiles, insects

Things to do at home before you leave
- [ ] Apply insect repellant to clothing
- [ ] Tell neighbors/friends:
  - Where you are going
  - Who the members of the groups are
  - How long you plan to be gone
  - What you are wearing and what supplies you have.
- [ ] Remember to report your safe return to them, too.
- [ ] Who to contact if you do not return.

GLOSSARY

Abdomen The rear body segment of an insect, spider, scorpion, or other arthropod.

Alga Any of a large group of organisms, mostly aquatic, that can produce food by photosynthesis, but lack true roots, stem, and leaves. Singular alga (AL ga); plural algae (AL gee)

Amphibians The group of animals that includes frogs, toads, spadefoots, salamanders, and newts. Their skins are moist and without scales. Amphibians require wet or moist conditions during all or a part of their lives. Most frogs and toads begin life as tadpoles, breathing underwater through gills, and later develop air-breathing lungs.

Animal Any living thing hat is not a plant, alga, fungus, or bacteria.

Annual A plant with a life span (seed to seed) of less than a year.

Arachnids The group of arthropods with four pairs of legs, two body parts (cephalothorax and abdomen), and no antennae that includes spiders, scorpions, mites, and ticks.

Arroyo A small canyon or gully with vertical sides and a flat bottom that was formed by rushing water. It is dry except after a heavy rain when it quickly becomes a fast moving river. Arroyo is Spanish for wash.

Arthropods Invertebrate animals with jointed legs, segmented body, and exoskeleton; includes insects, arachnids, crustaceans, centipedes, and millipedes.

Caliche (kuh LEE chee) A hard lime deposit commonly found in desert soils. The whitish-gray layers or rocks resemble cement. It is caused by the interaction between the acids contained in ancient rainfalls and the minerals within the soil.

Carapace The top shell of a tortoise or turtle.

Carnivore A meat-eater.

Chlorophyll The green pigment in plants that is necessary for plants to produce food. It enables a plant to use the energy from sunlight to convert carbon dioxide and water into carbohydrates.

Chubasco Severe storms that occur in late summer. They form over the Pacific, often a result of a hurricane or tropical storm, and can drop large amounts of rain on the Sonoran Desert.

Cochineal A small scale insect. It lives beneath the white, waxy coating found on some prickly pear and cholla cactus stems. The body of the female contains a bright red liquid which has been used as a dye.

Consumer An organism that eats other organisms.

Crepuscular Active at dusk or dawn.

Crustaceans The group of arthropods with hard exoskeleton; includes shrimp, crabs, and lobsters.

Cryptic Serving to conceal or camouflage.

Cryptobiotic soil Soil crust made up of tiny living organisms including algae, fungi, lichens, and mosses.

Dendrite Tree-like or branching patterns found on rocks; composed of mineral films such as manganese oxide.

Desert A place where free water is severely limited to plant and animal life most of the year.

Desert pavement A surface layer on the desert floor made of rocks or pebbles closely arranged, almost as if they were put together as a jigsaw puzzle.

Desert varnish A hard, dark, shiny coating on rocks, composed mainly of manganese; caused by biological actions over thousands of years.

Diurnal Active during the day.

Dormant A state of inactivity in plants or animals.

Ecosystem The interacting system of living organisms and non-living components in any given area.

Endothermic Producing heat from within the body. Birds and mammals are endothermic. "Warm-blooded" is often used instead, but "endothermic" is more accurate and scientific.

Erosion The wearing away and shifting of rock and soil by water, wind, and other forces.

Fauna Animals of a region

Field mark Any feature of an animal such as shape, color, or pattern, that helps in its identification.

Flora Plants of a region

Fungus An organism that cannot produce its own food and must therefore ingest other organic matter. A mushroom is one type of fungus. Singular fungus (FUN gus); plural fungi (FUN gee)

Gall A spherical growth on plant tissue caused by an insect, bacteria, or fungus.

Geology The study of the earth's crust (rocks, soil, land forms) and the changes that have occurred and are still occurring.

Germinate To sprout or begin to grow from a seed.

Glochids Tiny hair-like spines that surround the larger spines on prickly pear and cholla cactuses.

Gular horn The part of the lower shell of a tortoise that projects under the head ("gular" pertains to the throat).

Herbivore A plant-eater.

Host A plant or animal that supplies nourishment to another organism (parasite) living in or on it.

Igneous rock Rock formed from molten (melted) rock.

Larva The immature stage of animals that go through a major change in structure between the immature and adult forms. With insects, it is the stage of the life cycle between egg and pupa. The caterpillar is a larva of a moth or butterfly. A tadpole is a larva of a frog. (Plural larvae (LAR vay).

Lichen An organism made up of algae and fungi, living together in a condition called mutualism. It can have many colors including shades of green, blue-green, gray, orange, or yellow. It is often found on rocks but may grow on any surface that is suitable habitat.

Mammal A member of the group of animals that have backbones, hair or fur, are endothermic (warm-blooded), and where the female nurses the young with milk secreted from mammary glands. Humans are mammals.

Metamorphic rock Rock reformed from preexisting rocks by extreme heat, pressure, and underground forces.

Microhabitat A small habitat different from the larger habitat that surrounds it. Example a cool, moist, shady wash bank provides growing conditions for mosses and ferns that could not survive in the hot sunshine a short distance away.

Midden The accumulation of den building materials gathered by packrats which, over many years, is cemented together and preserved by urine.

Minerals Minerals are crystal structures and chemical compositions that make up a rock, just as flour, butter, eggs, and nuts mixed and baked are the ingredients of a cookie.

Monsoon An Arabic word that means a seasonal wind. In the Sonoran Desert we think of summer as the monsoon season when strong winds bring thunderstorms.

Mortar Any stone with a cup-shaped depression used to hold seeds or other materials for pounding and grinding. Mortars found in huge rocks, often along streambeds, are called bedrock mortars.

Mutualism The coexistence of two species in which both derive equal benefit and no harm from the association. Both species require the presence of the other to survive. Lichen is a good example.

Naiad (NAY ad) The immature, aquatic form of insects such as dragonflies and damselflies.

Nectar The sweet liquid within a flower that attracts insects and other animals.

Nectar guides The lines on flower petals which act as "lane markers" for insects. In the insects' eyes these lines stand out and guide them to the nectar within the flower.

Nocturnal Active during the night.

Nurse plant Any plant that provides protection from weather or predation for another plant growing beneath its branches.

Nopal The Spanish name for prickly pear cactus.

Nopalitos Sliced or diced prickly pear that is cooked and eaten as a vegetable.

Omnivore An animal that eats both plant and animal material.

Parasite Any species that lives in or on another organism (a host) and obtains some or all of its nourishment from the host.

Perennial A plant that lives for more than a year.

Pestle A rod-shaped stone tool used with a mortar to pound and grind seeds or other materials.

Petroglyphs Figures and symbols chipped into rock surfaces by prehistoric people. (Pictographs are images painted on rock.)

Photosynthesis The process in which green plants use the energy of sunlight to convert carbon dioxide and water into carbohydrates. The green pigment, chlorophyll, is the energy converter.

Pistil The female part of a flower. It produces seeds after fertilization by pollen from the male part of the flower, the stamens.

Plastron The bottom shell of a tortoise.

Pollen The powdery substance produced by the stamens (the male part of the flower) which is necessary for fertilization.

Pollination The process of fertilization within the flowers of plants, which produces reproductive seeds.

Pollinator Any animal or action that transfers the pollen from flower to flower resulting in fertilization.

Predaceous Predatory; preying on animals.

Producer An organism that produces food. Plants are producers.

Pupa The stage of an insect between the larval and the adult forms; during this time the insect makes many anatomical changes as it develops into the adult form. The cocoon of a moth is an example of a pupa. (Pupae - plural)

Rodent A member of a large group of gnawing animals including rats, mice, squirrels, beavers, and porcupines. Rodents have large constantly growing incisors (the four front teeth — two top and two bottom) usually yellow or red-brown in color.

Saguaro boot The boot- or shoe-shaped woody structure that was formed by scar tissue when a woodpecker carved out a nest cavity within a saguaro.

Scat Fecal (solid waste) material deposited by an animal.

Scute A bony or hard scale cover on reptiles (and some fish).

Sedimentary rock Rock composed of bits and pieces of older rocks that had been broken apart, moved by water, wind, or ice, then cemented together. These rocks may contain fossils.

Selaginella A spike moss which grows on north-facing slopes and other somewhat shaded areas. It is brown, dry, curled and appears dead during dry weather, but becomes soft and green within hours of a rain. It is also called resurrection plant.

Sepal One of the leaf-like, usually green, structures that envelops the outer base of a flower.

Sonoran Desert One of the four North American deserts. It covers much of southern and central Arizona, a bit of southeastern California, northeastern Sonora, Mexico, and most of the Baja California peninsula in Mexico.

Spine A modified leaf or part of a leaf in the form of a sharply pointed needle-like growth. Cactuses have spines.

Stamens The male parts of a flower. They produce the pollen which, when transferred to the pistil (the female part), fertilize the flower.

Succulent A plant or part of a plant which stores moisture. Storage may take place in leaves, stems, and/or roots.

Thorax The middle body segment of an insect. The three pairs of legs are attached to the thorax.

Thorn A sharply tipped, hard, woody projection on branches or tips of branches. Ocotillos, acacias, mesquites, and palo verdes have thorns.

Wash A desert streambed, dry most of the year, becoming a river after a rainstorm.

Wildlife corridor A natural passageway used by wildlife to access food, water, shelter, or migration routes.

INDEX